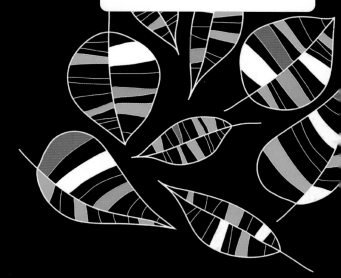

Grammar

to 14

Don Shiach

Consultant Editor: Geoff Barton

OXFORD
UNIVERSITY PRESS

Great Clarendon Street, Oxford OX2 6DP

Oxford University Press is a department of the University of Oxford.
It furthers the University's objective of excellence in research,
scholarship, and education by publishing worldwide in

Oxford   New York

Auckland   Cape Town   Dar es Salaam   Hong Kong   Karachi
Kuala Lumpur   Madrid   Melbourne   Mexico City   Nairobi
New Delhi   Shanghai   Taipei   Toronto

With offices in

Argentina   Austria   Brazil   Chile   Czech Republic   France   Greece
Guatemala   Hungary   Italy   Japan   Poland   Portugal   Singapore
South Korea   Switzerland   Thailand   Turkey   Ukraine   Vietnam

Oxford is a registered trade mark of Oxford University Press
in the UK and in certain other countries

British Library Cataloguing in Publication Data

Data available

ISBN 978-0-19-832111-8

10 9 8 7 6

Printed by Printplus, China.

Acknowledgements

Cover: Imrich Farkas/Dreamstime.com; **p15:** Chris Harvey/Shutterstock;
p17: sportgraphic/Shutterstock; **p23:** AISPIX/Shutterstock; **p25:** catlook/
Shutterstock; **p31:** Patrick Tuohy/Shutterstock; **p51:** Lars Christensen/
Shutterstock; **p75r:** Sandra Cunningham/Shutterstock; **p75l:** Simon
Krzic/Shutterstock; **p85:** Josemaria Toscano/Shutterstock; **p105:** RoxyFer/
Shutterstock (inset); **p105:** dwphotos/Shutterstock; **p133:** Photos 12/
Alamy; **p139:** ravl/Shutterstock; **p145:** George S de Blonsky/Alamy; **p151:**
antipathique/Shutterstock.

Illustrations are by Rory Walker, and Barking Dog Art.

Layout by Sharon Ryan.

Paper used in the production of this book is a natural, recyclable product
made from wood grown in sustainable forests. The manufacturing process
conforms to the environmental regulations of the country of origin.

Introduction

Grammar is a way of describing language. If you have a sound knowledge of the ways in which the English language works through its grammar, then you will be much more confident in how you use it to communicate in both speech and writing.

The aim of *Grammar to 14* is to help you communicate more effectively in English, firstly by understanding English grammar and knowing how to apply its rules, secondly by using punctuation accurately in your written work, and thirdly by spelling words correctly.

The book is divided into four main sections: Section 1 on Grammar, Section 2 on Punctuation, Section 3 on Spelling and Section 4 consisting of test questions.

Sections 1, 2, and 3 are divided into two-page units. Each of these offers a clear explanation of a particular aspect of grammar, punctuation or spelling with examples and illustrations. Every unit concludes with a series of follow-up activities which are graded for difficulty. 'Starting point' provides activities that test basic knowledge, 'Going further' includes activities at a higher level, and 'Further still' offers opportunities for more advanced work, often drawing together several points covered in a unit.

The test questions in Section 4 will help to show how much progress you have made in your understanding and usage of grammar, spelling and punctuation.

The accompanying Answer Book supplies all answers for activities and test questions in this book and further extension activities and test marking guidelines.

Grammar to 14 is a comprehensive aid to improving your knowledge and use of English grammar, punctuation and spelling. I hope you enjoy, and benefit from, using it.

Don Shiach

Contents

Section 2: Punctuation

Section 3: Spelling

Section 4: Test Questions

Index

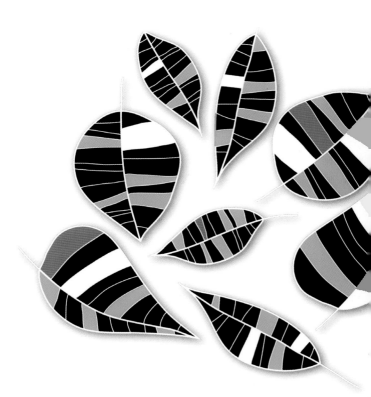

Nouns are the names we give to the things, places, feelings, thoughts, people, animals and qualities that make up our experience of the world. We use nouns to describe the difference between:

- one thing and another
- one person and another
- one feeling and another feeling
- one activity and another activity
- one place and another place
- one idea and another idea.

We explain and define the world around us by the many different nouns we use.

Common nouns

Common nouns name things, types of people, places and animals. They are usually the words we use to label things, people and animals that have a physical existence. These are all common nouns:

> face   seat   side   road   tickets   house   branch   cat
> accountant   woman   ruler   television   disc   table   hospital

They are called 'common' nouns because they make up the bulk of the nouns we use. They are the words we use to describe our physical surroundings in all its variety.

Proper nouns

Proper nouns are the actual names we give to particular people, places, organizations, products, days of the week, months, job titles and many other things. Proper nouns are not nouns that describe types of people and places, such as *solicitor*, *dancer*, *doctor*, *village*; they are the actual names of people, places and other things.

As they are names, proper nouns always begin with capital letters.

These are all proper nouns because they are the names of places:

> Kingston, Jamaica   Acacia Avenue   Manchester, England

These are all proper nouns because they are the names of people:

> Rafael Nadal   David Beckham   Helen Mirren
> Benjamin Zephaniah

These are all proper nouns because they are the names of organizations:

> Railtrack   Barnsley Football Club   Women's Hockey Association

These are all proper nouns because they are the names of days or months:

> Sunday   Tuesday   Saturday   January   May   July

These are all proper nouns because they are official titles:

> Prime Minister   Director of Education   President of France

Starting point

1 Pick out the common nouns in the following signs.

a Four oranges for a pound!

b Leave your bicycles here

c SEATS AT ALL PRICES

d ENTRANCE FOR VISITING SUPPORTERS

2 Pick out the proper nouns in the following headlines.

a Murray Wins in Triumph!

b Tuesday Replay for Arsenal

c Chief Inspector of Schools Praises Teachers

d Wettest June on Record!

Going further

1 Fill the gaps in these sentences with an appropriate common or proper noun.
   a It's a lovely _____ today!
   b I'm singing in the _____ !
   c Cash in your _____ at the _____ .
   d My favourite month is _____ , says superstar _____ _____ .
   e _____ _____ is my favourite film star.

2 Pick out the nouns in the following headlines and say whether they are common or proper nouns.

a Litter Is Spoiling Countryside, Says Prime Minister

b Tigers Still Survive in Africa

c Players in Australia are Better, Claims Coach

d Price of Houses in Wales Increase

Further still

Fill in the gaps in the following passage with an appropriate common or proper noun. Try not to use the same noun twice.

_____ _____ , the famous _____ , has just completed her latest novel. Her many _____ will be delighted by this latest _____ and her publishers, _____ and _____ , are looking forward to massive _____ . The irrepressible _____ will be travelling the length and breadth of _____ and _____ to publicize her _____ .

Abstract Nouns and Collective Nouns

Abstract nouns

Abstract nouns name feelings, qualities and ideas, and 'things' that have no physical existence. They describe things you cannot touch but which you can feel, think or experience.

In each of the following sentences, the abstract nouns are in italics.

> I felt an intense *hunger*.
> Their *joy* was overwhelming.
> Your *failure* gives me no *satisfaction*.
> We have to come up with some new *ideas*!

Just as common nouns help to describe the physical world around us, abstract nouns help to describe the nonphysical 'things' that matter to us: our feelings, thoughts, hopes, needs and ambitions.

Collective nouns

Collective nouns are the names given to groups of people, animals or things which are seen as a whole or as a group. Collective nouns do not refer to individual people or animals but to particular classes of people or animals.

The words in italics in the following sentences are all examples of collective nouns.

> A *crowd* of onlookers gathered at the scene of the accident.
> The *herd* of elephants ambled by the water.
> A *flock* of birds flew towards the pier.
> The interviewing *panel* took a long time over their decision.

Other examples of collective nouns are:

> team   committee   squadron   group   mob
> gaggle   swarm   pride (of lions)

Starting point

1 Pick out the abstract nouns in the following sentences:
a My ambition is to become a dancer.
b She expressed her anger to the supervisor.
c Faith, hope and charity are three of the virtues.

2 Identify collective nouns in the following headlines:
a

Housing Estate Needs Improvements

b

Police Squad Crack Case

c

Teams of Investigators Assigned To Case

Going further

Choose an appropriate abstract or collective noun for each gap in these sentences.

a 'I have given up all _____ ,' stated _____ captain, Althea Norman.

b The _____ of birds was migrating to its winter quarters.

c 'The sighting of the creature was pure _____ ,' claimed the general.

d The _____ of seeing the _____ of kittens for the first time was immeasurable.

e _____ of flying stops whole _____ of people from travelling by air.

Further still

Read the following passage and pick out the abstract and collective nouns. Make two lists under the two headings: Abstract and Collective.

Interest in the success of the team is incredible. The population of whole areas have formed supporters' clubs and committees have been elected to organize events. The hope of all the groups is to see their team play in the Cup Final. 'For every true fan, that is their greatest ambition,' stated the secretary of one large organization.

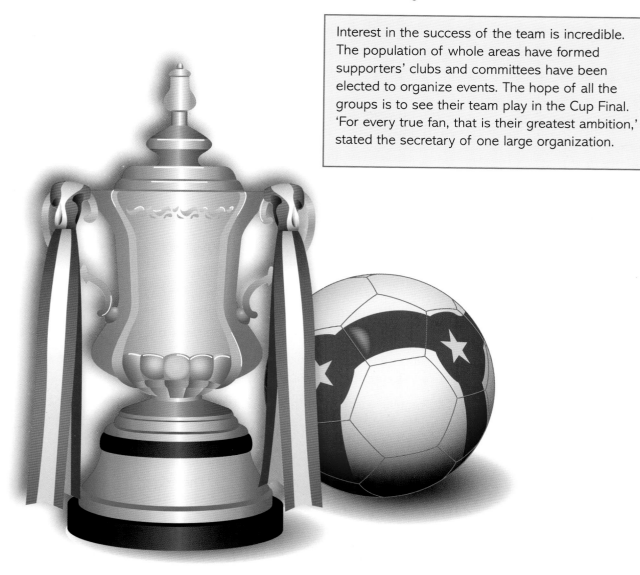

Regular Verbs

What are verbs?   **Verbs** often tell us about the actions people or things do or have done:

> We *close* the doors.

Verbs sometimes tell us about feelings that are being or have been felt:

> I *feel* very sad.

Verbs may be about existing, being, appearing or becoming:

> She *appears* to be very happy.   I *am becoming* very despondent.

A verb may consist of more than one word (e.g. *am becoming* in the example above). We can refer to the verb element in a sentence or a clause as the **verb phrase**. In verbs that consist of more than one word, there is at least one 'helping' or **auxiliary verb**: *He could have been resting*. The main verb is *resting*, *could have been* are all helping or auxiliary verbs. Together they make up the verb phrase in the sentence. We will return to auxiliary verbs on page 14.

Regular verbs   Verbs divide into two main kinds: regular or irregular. **Regular verbs** obey the same rules as hundreds of other verbs in forming their present and past tenses and also in forming present and past participles.

First, however, let us consider the verb in its basic form, i.e. the form of the verb that has not been altered by tense or person. For example:

> cook   imagine   seem   laugh   cry

When we refer to the **infinitive**, we mean this basic form of the verb with the word 'to' in front of it:

> to cook   to imagine   to seem   to laugh   to cry

We can now look at the rules that regular verbs obey when their form is altered from the basic form.

1 Regular verbs form their present tense by adding *-s* to the basic form when the person is third person singular (he, she, it):

> He *cooks* the meal.   She *imagines* the worst.   It *seems* to be fine.

All other persons (they, we) keep to the basic form of the verb:

> They *cook* the meal.   We *imagine* the worst.

2 Regular verbs form their past tense by adding *-ed* to the basic form. (But note that verbs that end in *-e* add only *-d* and verbs that end in *-y* change to *-ie* and add *-d*.)

> I *cooked* the meal.   You *imagined* wonderful visions.
>
> We *laughed* at every joke.   They *cried* because of the result.

This rule of adding *-ed* to the basic form of the verb applies to all three persons of the past tense, both singular and plural. (For more on person and tense see pages 42 and 18.)

3 Regular verbs also form their participles in a uniform way. Participles are the *-ing* and *-ed* forms created from the basic verb.

The present participle is the *-ing* form and is used in the continuous present tense:

> I am *reading* this book.

This expresses an action that is continuing and has not been completed yet. Present participles are also used in participial phrases and as adjectives:

> *Looking* back on it now, it was a very *surprising* result.

The past participle is the *-ed* form. It can also be used in participial phrases or as an adjective:

> *Surprised* by the verdict, he decided to appeal.
> I bought some *cooked* meat.

Starting point

1 Write down the third person singular form in the present tense of the following regular verbs:

burn   light   mean   exist   fear   donate   meet   leave

2 Use four of the answers you have given for question 1 and write a sentence for each of them.

3 Write down the past tense of the following regular verbs:

discover   paint   listen   list   clean   try
swop   miss   mark   hate   emphasize   marry

4 Use four of the answers you have given for question 3 and write a separate sentence for each.

Going further

Fill in the gaps in each of the following advertising slogans with a suitable regular verb in its correct form.

a He _____ the day with Banana-Pops!
b You can't _____ an egg!
c The Western, the bank that _____ its customers.
d Purrfect, the cat food that cats simply _____ !
e The Magic Galaxy Game _____ hours of pleasure and you _____ as well!

Further still

Write down the main verbs used in the following article under one heading and any infinitive forms under another heading.

Television caters enough for young people's tastes. With the vast increase in the number of channels available, it is difficult not to argue that young people have a great variety of programmes to watch.

Advertisers realize that they reach young people with their products through popular programmes, which, some people argue, encourages youngsters to want unnecessary things.

Irregular Verbs

Many verbs do not obey the rules that regular verbs follow. These are called **irregular verbs**.

There is only one way of knowing irregular verbs from regular verbs: you have to make yourself familiar with the special forms that irregular verbs take when they alter from the basic form of the verb because of person and/or tense.

Probably the most commonly used verb in English is the verb *to be*. Yet it is an irregular verb. Here are the altered forms of the verb:

Basic verb	Present tense	Past tense	Past participle
be	am/is/are	was/were	been

Other common irregular verbs

Here are the altered forms of the following common irregular verbs:

go	goes	went	gone
have	has	had	had
see	sees	saw	seen
give	gives	gave	given
know	knows	knew	known
think	thinks	thought	thought
speak	speaks	spoke	spoken
take	takes	took	taken

Patterns can be detected in groups of verbs that look or sound the same:

swim	swims	swam	swum
ring	rings	rang	rung
begin	begins	began	begun

But then the verb *bring* has a slightly different pattern:

bring	brings	brought	brought

Verbs that end in -*sh* or -*ch* add -*es* in the present third-person singular:

wash/washes   wish/wishes   reach/reaches

They usually have regular past tense and past participle forms but again there are exceptions:

teach	teaches	taught	taught
catch	catches	caught	caught

There is a recognizable pattern to the irregular verbs *break*, *wake*, *blow* and *throw*:

Basic verb	Present tense	Past tense	Past participle
break	breaks	broke	broken
wake	wakes	woke	woken
blow	blows	blew	blown
throw	throws	threw	thrown

Here are some more very common irregular verbs:

keep	keeps	kept	kept
meet	meets	met	met
shut	shuts	shut	shut
forget	forgets	forgot	forgotten
eat	eats	ate	eaten
fall	falls	fell	fallen

Starting point

In each of the following sentences, there are one or more examples of irregular verbs that have been incorrectly used. Pick out these errors and correct them.

a I taked only what I needed.
b We were telled that we had speaken out of turn.
c The speaker begun the meeting and breaked the silence.
d They been angry that the money had been stealen.
e She knowed the person who sended the message.
f The advisors gived instructions about how it should be spended.

Going further

In the following extract, the basic form of irregular verbs is shown in brackets. Write down the appropriate form of these verbs for their use in the extract.

Last year we (swim) _____ the channel. We (think) _____ we (have) _____ every chance of success, but we (meet) _____ unexpected difficulties. Although we (choose) _____ a clear day for the attempt, we (fall) _____ prey to bad weather because the wind (blow) _____ strongly and (drive) _____ us almost backwards in the water. In fact, the storm (catch) _____ us totally unaware, but somehow we (keep) _____ going, although soon all our energies were (spend) _____ . We (forget) _____ one basic rule. We had not (know) _____ enough about the conditions.

Further still

Write down the past tense and past participle forms of the following irregular verbs.

grow   write   bring   spin   sleep   run   cling   leave
forsake   forgive   overthrow   lose   ride   dig   freeze   forbid

Auxiliary Verbs in Verb Phrases

Read these advertising slogans:

Have You Brushed Your Teeth Today?

We are building for YOUR future.

Do you want to be really special?

The verb phrases in the slogans are *Have… brushed, are building* and *Do… want*. These verb phrases consist of an auxiliary verb plus the main verb:

> *have* (auxiliary verb) plus *brushed* (main verb)
>
> *are* (auxiliary verb) plus *building* (main verb)
>
> *do* (auxiliary verb) plus *want* (main verb)

Be, have and do

The verbs *to be*, *to have* and *to do* are verbs in their own right, but they are very often used to indicate tenses in other verbs, the difference between singular and plural, and questions – when they are 'added' to the main verb in the verb phrase.

> We *are enjoying* a great holiday.

In this sentence, the first person plural of the present tense of the verb *to be* (*are*) is joined to the present participle of the main verb (*enjoying*) to form the verb phrase of the sentence: *are enjoying*.

> *Have* you *lost* your mind?

In this sentence, the second person singular of the present tense of the verb *to have* (*have*) is an auxiliary verb in the verb phrase: *Have... lost*.

> *Do* you *have* the right *to ask* me that?

In this sentence, *do* is an auxiliary verb and helps the main verb, *to ask*, to pose a question in the verb phrase: *Do... have*. Remember that verb phrases very often consist of two, three or four words to indicate tense, number or a question.

Other auxiliary verbs

Other auxiliary verbs are:

may	might	will	would	shall	should
can	could	must	used (to)	need	ought (to)

These are called **modal auxiliaries** because they show a degree of judgement about what is being done. These verbs do not exist in their own right as main verbs.

> I *may* have to change my plans. It *might* rain today, so that *will* spoil our trip. We *shall* have to think about what to do, because we *must* not waste the day.

Starting point

Here are some auxiliary verbs:

do   have   should   would

may   might   have   can   could

Read the following sentences. With a partner or on your own, decide which of these auxiliary verbs would fit into the gaps and make sense.

a _____ you remember the fifth of November?
b There_____ be trouble ahead.
c _____ you bought any bananas today?
d There's no point in thinking about what _____ _____ been.
e I_____ go, if you_____ just say the word.
f I_____ do my homework, because there_____ be an exam tomorrow.
g _____ you ever been to Trinidad?

Going further

Read the following passage. You are given several choices of auxiliary verbs within a verb phrase. Choose the correct auxiliary in each case.

> The test match can/could have been played, if the weather have/had been slightly better, but the rain were/was falling in the early morning and the ground staff should/could not do anything about it. The spectators were/was showing great patience, as most of them do/would have paid a lot for their tickets. Has/Do the cricket authorities have any solution to the problem? Would/Shall/Should people have their money returned if there is very little play? Does/Have the spectator have some rights? After all, cricket should/could not continue without people paying to watch.

Further still

Read the following news report. Pick out the errors in the use of auxiliary verbs in the verb phrases and correct them. You will either need to alter the tense of the verb or to replace it completely with a more appropriate auxiliary.

NEWS ON-LINE **SOUTH**

Holiday-makers was going about the business of enjoying themselves at Brighton yesterday, when what may happen but a real-life adventure. A pleasure boat, which have been blown off-shore, were having difficulties. There can be only one solution: there need to be a daring rescue. But might the lifeboat crew be assembled quickly? The answer should not has been clearer. Anxious spectators might only watch as the boat had launched. The winds may not but hamper their progress, but bravely they was sticking to their task. Finally, everyone did breathe easily again. The daring mission have been accomplished.

Subject–verb Agreement

The **subject** of a sentence or a clause is usually a noun or a pronoun which carries out the action (the verb). In the following sentences, the words in italics are the subjects:

1 *She* was very happy.
2 *The authorities* were concerned at the news of budget cuts.
3 *You* will be amused by this joke.
4 *I* am very pleasantly surprised by the result.

The verb has to change its form to agree with its subject. Agreement is made according to the number and person of the subject. A closer look at the agreements made in the examples above will show how this works.

In sentence 1, *She* is the subject of the verb *was*. *She* is third person singular, the tense is the past tense of the verb 'to be', thus *She was* is the correct form, agreeing the verb with its subject.

In sentence 2, *authorities* is the subject of the verb *were concerned*. This time the number is plural, the person is third and the tense is the past.

In sentence 3, *You* is the subject of the verb *will be amused*. The person is second, it could be either singular or plural and the tense is future.

In sentence 4, *I* is the subject of the verb *am*. The person is the first person singular and the tense is the present tense.

Subject–verb agreement tips	Tricky agreements

There are some tricky subject–verb agreements that you need to be aware of. Be careful with compound or combined subjects. They take a plural verb.

> *The father and son* resemble one another.

On the other hand, some subjects look as though they are plural, when they are in fact singular:

> *One* of the cars developed engine trouble.
> *A choice* of main courses is available.

In both these sentences a plural noun (*cars* and *courses*) is positioned next to the verb, but the verb is to be singular because the actual subjects are singular (*one* and *choice*).

When the normal word order in a sentence is turned around or inverted, care has to be taken about subject–verb agreement:

> Towering high in the sky are these huge office *buildings*.

The subject is *buildings*, not *sky* which appears next to the verb due to the inversion. So the verb agrees with its plural subject.

Collective nouns usually take singular verbs:

> *A flock* of sheep is crossing the road.
> *The government* has promised to reduce taxes.

(For more on person and subjects see pages 42 and 66.)

Starting point

For each of the gaps in the following sentences, decide on a verb that would fit. Make sure that there is correct subject–verb agreement.

a Cats _____ loyal pets and _____ their owners lots of affection.
b We _____ very happy with the result of the game.
c One of his sister's CDs _____ broken and he knew who _____ it.
d I _____ having to do my homework.
e They _____ exercise and definitely _____ daily runs.

Going further

1 Read the following sentences and decide whether the subject–verb agreements are correct or incorrect. Where you think there are errors, make the appropriate correction.

a He and I is always in agreement over this matter.
b Although the range of clothes was extensive, neither Jane nor Mark were in the buying mood.
c The number of people attending the fair have increased.
d The sound of music was heard in the distance, even though the group of musicians were performing miles away.

2 Find the errors in subject–verb agreement in these sentences. In each case explain the cause of the error.

a You and your partner deserves the best.
b One of us are wrong!
c A flock of birds roost in nearby trees.
d A range of flavours are available.
e The whole family are meeting up.
f The audience were not clapping.

Further still

In the following report, there are a number of errors in the agreements between subjects and verbs. Identify these and provide the correct versions.

Footie Frenzy

The Nunthorpe players was not downhearted by their recent cup defeat. Joe Ellis, the captain, have spoken for all the team when he said that they would be trying for the trophy again next year. He congratulated the supporters who was magnificent. Neither the manger nor he himself were feeling downcast and they was all looking forward to next season. Each of the team members were keen to challenge for the title next season. Everybody were confident.

Verb Tenses

Verbs, apart from the infinitive form, always give an indication of time, whether it is present, past or future. Verbs or verb phrases have to alter their forms to show time and we call this the **verb tense**.

The present and continuous present tense

The **present tense** is used to indicate something that is happening now. There are two forms of the present tense, which have slightly different meanings.

The -*s* ending in regular verbs, and many irregular verbs as well, shows present time:

> He *drives* to the market each day.
>
> He *wakes* up early every morning.

Both of these examples indicate repeated actions that happen regularly in the present.

The other form of the present tense is called the **continuous present**:

> I *am studying*, so please don't interrupt.
>
> We *are staying* at that hotel.

These examples indicate actions that are happening in the present but are not complete. The actions are continuing and this is why this form of the present tense is referred to as the continuous present.

The past and continuous past tense

The **past tense** in regular verbs is the -*ed* form:

> I *knocked*.   They *shouted*.

Irregular verbs have their own form of the past tense, which you should become familiar with. (See page 12.)

The ordinary past tense indicates the time of an action that has been completed:

> I *completed* the essay that evening.

The **continuous past** indicates past time, but describes an action in the past that has not yet been completed:

> I *was walking* along the road, when I met an old friend.

The future tense

Auxiliary verbs are needed to form the **future tense** in verb phrases. The auxiliary verbs that are used include:

> will   shall   am/is/are going to   may   am/is/are about to

I will is often contracted to *I'll*:

> I *will* see you tomorrow then.
>
> I'll see you tomorrow then.

Shall is an alternative to *will*:

> We *shall* see you tomorrow.

Very often, however, *shall* indicates determination as well as future tense:

> I *shall* succeed even if it kills me.

Here are some examples of other auxiliary verbs used in verb phrases to indicate future time:

> I *am* going to tell him off as soon as possible.
>
> I *may* visit them next week.
>
> They *are* about to make a decision.

Starting point

Read the following sentences and identify whether the verb phrases used are in the present, past or future tense.

a I am reading this newspaper because I like it.

b I will leave town tomorrow, because I am bored.

c I was whistling a tune, but I didn't know the title.

d I strode down the road and I passed him before long.

e I am about to eat my dinner, so I will phone you back.

f I forgot to lock the door, so I am afraid we may be robbed.

Going further

What verb tense is used in each of these sentences?

a Vishal runs 5km every night.

b We will have an amazing time at the festival.

c She was panicking about the exams, when the solution became clear.

d I'm going to Barcelona on holiday this year.

e Terrified, Steven crept silently down the corridor.

f We have to find a new venue for the gig next week.

Further still

The following passage is written in the present tense. Change all the verbs and verb phrases into the past tense.

I am walking down some mean streets. The city is quiet. All the bad guys are in bed asleep, I am thinking. But it is too quiet. Something is not quite right. Suddenly, I hear something behind me. A man in an overcoat and trilby hat runs round the corner. He sees me and stops. He looks frightened and seems to be asking for my help. I gesture towards an alleyway near him. He disappears down it. Seconds later, a second man appears. He does not look pleased to see me. The feeling is mutual.

Participles of the Verb

Present participles

The **present participle** is the -*ing* form and is used in the continuous present tense:

> I am read*ing* this book.   He is think*ing* it over.

This expresses an action that is continuing and has not been completed yet. (See page 18.)

Phrases using the present participle of a verb

The present participle of a verb can be used in a participial phrase:

> *Dreaming* of adventures that lay ahead, I found I was no longer listening.

But you have to be careful to relate the participle to the subject of the sentence, otherwise it might not be clear what you mean:

> *Walking* along the road, the cinema appeared on the right.

This makes it seem like *the cinema* is walking along the road! This is an example of a **misrelated participle.** This sentence needs to be reconstructed like this:

> *Walking* along the road, we saw the cinema appear on the right.

The following sentence clearly links the participle to the subject of the clause that follows:

> *Realizing* my error, *I* tried to correct it.

A participial phrase can also come after the subject it qualifies:

> *The man*, *making* an instant decision, nodded his head.

Phrases using the past participle of a verb

The **past participle** of regular verbs ends in -*ed*:

> *Surprised* by the nightwatchman's entrance, the burglars fled the building.

Again, past participles are very useful in phrases that can be added to sentences to give further information:

> *Astonished* by her reaction, he quickly changed his tune.
>
> The salesman, *angered* by the customer's rudeness, walked away.

Having and *being* are also useful participles to use. Note that *having* almost always has to be used with a participle of another verb.

> *Having been* taught well, I had no problem with maths.
>
> He, *being* the brave man he was, rescued the child.
>
> The policewoman, *having directed* traffic all day, took a well-earned rest.

Starting point

1 Choose the most appropriate participle from this list to fill in each of the gaps in the following sentences:

singing   having   leaving   sensing   bewildered

a _____ the dance, I caught a bus home.

b _____ eaten my fill, I excused myself from the table.

c The lion, _____ the approach of his prey, crouched low in the grass.

d _____ by the confusion, we decided to wait till things had calmed down.

e _____ loudly, the team celebrated its victory.

Going further

1 Complete the following sentences with an appropriate participial phrase.

a (_____), they left thankfully for home.

b The protestors, (_____), decided to call it a day.

c (_____), the gardener took the rubbish to the dump.

d The ice-cream van, (_____), drove round the town.

2 Read the following passage and fill in each gap with an appropriate participial phrase.

The visitors, (_____), were popular with their supporters. However, the home team, (_____), fought back. Within ten minutes, they had equalized, (_____). Victory beckoned and the home team, (_____), redoubled its efforts. Just before half-time, they scored again, their main striker who was a recent signing, (_____).

Further still

In the following passage, there are several incorrect uses of present and past participles, including some examples of misrelated participles. Pick these errors out and correct them either by using the correct participle or by rewriting the sentence completely.

Riding along on my bicycle, the hill suddenly loomed up in front of me. Surprising by its steepness, I decided to dismount and walk. Mark, been the show-off he is, passed me when I was halfway up. Pedalled furiously, I caught up with him. He, been the competitive person he is, redoubled his effort, convincing that he could beat me. Delighting by his small triumph, he made a gesture of victory, while I panting for breath.

Adjectives

Adjectives are describing words. They are used to describe nouns or pronouns. Adjectives give us additional information about things, places, people, qualities or ideas.

In the following extract, the words in italics are all adjectives:

> The *golden* sun was *high* in the *blue* sky. The *intense* heat was not *unpleasant*, however, because it was not *humid* and *cloying* and anyway there was a *delightful*, *light*, *cooling* and extremely *welcome* breeze that fanned her *glowing* cheeks.
>
> She looked towards the *distant* and *mysterious* hills. Beyond *that far* horizon lay the *beautiful*, *fantastic* city of *her* dreams.

You can use adjectives in your writing to make it more vivid and varied.

The positioning of adjectives

Notice that adjectives may come immediately before the noun they describe or they may come after the verb and therefore be detached from the noun or pronoun they are describing:

> The *intense* heat was not *unpleasant*…

Adjectives before a noun or after a verb may come in twos or threes for effect.

> …there was a *delightful*, *light*, *cooling* and extremely *welcome* breeze.

Note that a comma is placed between each adjective in a string.

Adjective tips

Adding detail to your writing

Adjectives can add interesting detail to a piece of writing but, beware, as you can easily overdo them by piling one on top of another. For example, the last sentence in the extract above definitely contains one adjective too many.

It is not a matter of how many adjectives you can use, but how effective they are in adding vivid detail to your writing.

Try also to think of less familiar adjectives than some of these:

nice   beautiful   boring   lovely   awful   bad   marvellous

There is nothing wrong with any of these words, except that they are often overused. The result can be that they lose some of their impact.

Starting point

1 Pick out the adjectives used in the following newspaper headlines.

a Athletics Reaches New Low Point

b HUGE INCREASE IN CRIME FIGURES

c New Film Is Amazing Box-office Success!

d BRITISH PLAYER A HERO!

e Dreadful Mess Must Be Cleared Up!

f WAY OUT FOR EMBATTLED MINISTER

2 Read the following diary entry and pick out the adjectives that are used.

NOVEMBER 25TH

Late start to a grey day. Quick walk to school and then a hilarious experiment in Science that went wrong. I had hockey practice at lunchtime. We've got a difficult match next week. Then home for my favourite tea and the usual homework.

Going further

Read the following article and pick out six adjectives. Write them out along with the noun they describe.

Dynamic Rise

Tempestuous new rock group, 'The Dynamics', are set to break all records when they play their gig at the splendid Market Hall venue. These musicians are not only talented but have a natural instinct for sheer showmanship that marks them down for instantaneous stardom. Lead singer, Olivia, has genuine charisma and will no doubt soon have endless, devoted fans. Watch this space for the 'dynamic' rise of this amazing group.

Further still

Read the following text from an advertisement in which gaps have been left for appropriate adjectives. Choose an adjective for each gap that adds to the persuasive effect of the advertisement.

Elite chocolates are quite _____ .
Not only are they _____ , but they are not _____ . Impress your guests by handing round these _____ concoctions after dinner. _____ taste, a _____ price, _____ packaging: it all adds up to an _____ experience in chocolate eating.
Elite, the _____ name in confectionery.

Other Kinds of Adjective

Demonstrative adjectives

Demonstrative adjectives define which thing or things, person or persons are being spoken or written about. In the following newspaper headlines and advertising slogans, the words *this*, *that*, *these* and *those* are demonstrative adjectives.

That Performance Was Terrible!

This Game Has To Be Won!

These Bargains Have To Be Seen To Be Believed!

Those Fabulous Faces Are Back Again On Your Screens!

Be aware of the difference between these words when they are attached to a noun as adjectives and when they are used on their own as demonstrative pronouns, as in these examples:

This is your life!   *That's* the ticket!

Those were the days!   *These* are just the best!

Possessive adjectives

Possessive adjectives indicate ownership:

I love *my* Koyota!   *Your* kind of car is *our* kind of car.

Tom Webb in *his* greatest role…   *Her* ambition knew no bounds!

Our promises are made to be kept!   *Their* tragedy touches us all.

These examples show that possessive adjectives have to be attached to a noun to be classed as an adjective.

Interrogative adjectives

Interrogative adjectives are attached to nouns and ask questions, such as *which*, *whose* or *what* questions:

Which lesson have we got next?

Whose book is this?

What kind of question is that?

Note that *which*, *whose* and *what* can also stand on their own, unattached to a noun. Here they act as pronouns.

Which do you prefer?

What is the right thing to do?

Whose is this?

Other adjectives

These words are classed as adjectives only when attached to nouns:

all   any   each   either   neither   every   no   own

All hands on deck!   *Any* old iron!

Each person to his or her own taste.   *Either* choice will do.

Every day is a new beginning.   *Neither* party will win.

Do you want to own your *own* house?   *No* man is an island.

Starting point

1 Decide which demonstrative adjective (this, that, those, these) could fill each gap in the following sentences.

a _____ trainer is the best training shoe on the market.

b _____ brand is not so good.

c _____ trainers are not quite so trendy and as for _____ shoes, forget it!

2 Fill in the gaps in the following sentences with an appropriate possessive adjective.

a _____ dreams came true!

b Favourite ran _____ best ever race.

c Pensioners have to vacate _____ home.

d Forget _____ troubles right now!

Going further

Decide which interrogative adjective (which, whose or what) makes sense in the following sentences.

a _____ twin has used our shampoo?

b _____ car is right out in front?

c _____ type of computer game do most people like?

Further still

Read the following restaurant review. Pick out all the demonstrative, possessive and interrogative adjectives, listing them under the appropriate headings.

This dish was exquisite. Its flavour was very subtle and when we sampled it, our taste buds went wild. Which other chicken dish could produce that reaction? Its origin belongs to no one cook, but to my amazement it seems that one small Caribbean island deserves all these compliments.

Adverbs

A verb tells us about actions and feelings, or being and becoming. **Adverbs** are usually, but not always, attached to verbs and give additional information about them. They qualify the meaning of verbs, for example, by showing how an action is carried out.

Read the following extract. The words in italics are all adverbs.

> The car moved *slowly* through the fog. Luke stared *uncertainly* into the darkness. He had been *extremely* busy that day. He had finished one case and then *unexpectedly* he had received a call from a stranger who had *mysteriously* asked him to meet her at an address in the Hollywood Hills.

Notice how most of these adverbs are next, or close, to the verb in the sentence:

> The car moved *slowly* through the fog.

> Luke stared *uncertainly* into the darkness.

But sometimes adverbs can be placed elsewhere in the sentence, as long as it is clear to which verb they are attached:

> …then *unexpectedly* he had received a call…

The adverbs in the extract above add detail to the description and help to build up a mysterious atmosphere. The writing would be quite bland without them.

Adverbs with adjectives and other adverbs

Adverbs, however, may also qualify the meaning of adjectives or even other adverbs. For example, here the adverb *justifiably* adds to the meaning of the adjective *tired*:

> Luke was *justifiably* tired.

Here an adverb qualifies the meaning of another adverb:

> Who had left that car *so carelessly* parked in the middle of the road?

The adverb *so* qualifies the meaning of another adverb *carelessly*. Thus, although adverbs are usually attached to verbs, they can also be attached to adjectives and to other adverbs.

Recognizing adverbs and how they are formed

Most adverbs are formed by adding *-ly* to an adjective:

> magnificent/magnificent*ly*   sure/sure*ly*   frank/frank*ly*

But adjectives that end in *-y* usually drop the *-y*, replace it with *-i* and then add *-ly*:

> hungry/hungr*ily*   lazy/laz*ily*   happy/happ*ily*

Adjectives that end in *-le* drop the final *-e* and add *-y*:

> simple/simp*ly*   terrible/terrib*ly*   miserable/miserab*ly*

Starting point

1 Fill in the gaps in the following sentences with the most appropriate adverb from this list:

cheaply   fantastically   dangerously   magnificently   outrageously

a Do you want to insure your car _____ ?
b Our team played _____ !
c Teenager Drove _____ Through Crowded Streets.
d _____ Reduced Prices!
e Students Behaved _____ in Town Centre.

2 Pick out the adverbs in the following sentences that qualify an adjective or another adverb.
a That was simply unbelievable!
b They performed so magnificently!
c This was truly memorable.
d These exam results reflect very well on the school.

Going further

Choose appropriate adverbs to fill the gaps in the following sentences.

a I was _____ surprised that he passed the exam _____ , but _____ he had studied _____ without my knowing it.
b The movie started _____ , but it deteriorated _____ and soon I was _____ asleep and _____ awoke in time to see the ending.
c The group played _____ _____ , and the neighbours reacted _____ to this, although up to that point negotiations had proceeded _____ _____ .
d Drive _____ _____ round the corner and stop _____ you see the house.
e She was an _____ tall person and _____ she walked _____ towards him.
f He gazed at the treasure _____ and she decided _____ to make sure the jewels were returned _____ to their rightful owners.

Further still

Read this extract from an article and write down all the adverbs that are used.

Fortunately, the festival, which had been planned so meticulously, was not badly interrupted by the heavy rain. The organizers reluctantly had to cancel some events, but the crowds were very enthusiastic and the alterations did not substantially interfere with their enjoyment. Surprisingly, the uncertain weather did not affect the festival too heavily and it was immediately clear that the day had been spent profitably.

Different Types of Adverb

The adverbs considered in the previous unit are adverbs of manner. **Adverbs of manner** tell us something about how something is done. However, there are other types of adverb.

Adverbs of degree, time or place

Numerous adverbs do not end in -*ly*:

about	almost	enough	far	fast	here	much
more	most	never	not	perhaps	quite	rather
so	soon	sometimes	there	twice	very	well

These adverbs, which do not end in -*ly*, are usually adverbs of degree, time or place. But, as with every rule, there are always exceptions:

immediately   really   annually

Adverbs of degree tell us about the degree to which an action was performed or a feeling was experienced:

I was *so* angry.

He was *very* late.

The performance of the orchestra was *much* improved.

Adverbs of time tell us about the time of an action:

The concert is bound to commence *soon*.

Now is the time for action.

Adverbs of place tell us about where an action takes place:

The accident happened *there*.

Collect those books and tidy them away in *here*.

Adverbs for emphasis

Some adverbs are particularly useful for enforcing a point:

She was *definitely* telling the truth. *Certainly*, he wanted to defend her. He told her the verdict would *assuredly* be in their favour. *Surely* there could be no doubt about that. *Unfortunately*, there was a doubt.

Other adverbs express doubt:

We might *possibly* win, but most *probably* we won't. *Maybe* the team isn't good enough. *Perhaps* that is the truth.

Starting point

1 Pick out the adverbs of degree in these headlines.

a ‘I AM SO DISGUSTED,’ SAYS STAR

b ‘WE PLAYED VERY BADLY’ ADMITS MANAGER

c ‘THE COUNTRY MUST DO SO MUCH BETTER’ STATES MINISTER

2 Identify the adverbs of time in the following headlines.

a

> BENEFITS TO BE WITHDRAWN IMMEDIATELY

b

> GOVERNMENT NOW ADMITS ERROR

c

> TRAVEL TO MARS SOON

3 Find the adverbs of place in the following headlines.

a

> STARS LANDED HERE

b

> THEY WANT YOU OVER THERE!

c

> UNITED FALL BEHIND IN SECOND HALF

Going further

Read the following article and make a list of all the adverbs. Explain which type of adverb each belongs to, i.e. is it an adverb of manner, degree, time or place, or an adverb that expresses an emphasis or doubt.

CLUB BEHAVED OUTRAGEOUSLY, SAYS SACKED MANAGER

Bert Owen, the ex-manager of Tampala United, claimed yesterday that the club had treated him extremely shoddily in their manner of sacking him. 'Maybe I've been living in a quite different world,' said Owen, 'but I believe people should be treated decently, especially when they have served a club loyally for years, as I certainly have here.' When will he sue? 'I don't know,' he replied passionately, 'but I'm definitely going to do so.'

Further still

1 Read the following opening to a story. Choose four of the adverbs used and say what each of them adds to the meaning and the atmosphere.

> The fog had mysteriously settled in mid-morning. People were rather surprised because they had definitely been expecting another sunny day. There was something very nasty about this fog. People choked exasperatedly and looked balefully at the darkness. They turned bad-temperedly on the weather forecasters. 'They never get it right,' people said crossly.

2 Write the next paragraph using adverbs to add interest and detail.

Pronouns

Pronouns are words that may take the place of nouns. They are the 'stand-ins' of English grammar. If something has already been mentioned in a sentence, the next time it is referred to, a pronoun may be used in its place. This helps to avoid unnecessary repetition. However, it must be clear what the pronoun refers to. Read this extract from an advert for a new car:

> The Gaudi is a sleek, fast saloon car. *It* has a terrific maximum cruising speed. An added bonus is that *it* is economical on fuel as well.

The name of the car is mentioned in the first sentence. The pronoun *it* then may be safely used at the beginning of the second sentence because it is clear what *it* is 'standing in' for: *the Gaudi*. In the third sentence, *it* is used again as a pronoun standing in for the same noun. Consider how the advert would have read if the pronoun had not been used:

> The Gaudi is a sleek, fast saloon car. The Gaudi has a terrific maximum cruising speed. An added bonus is that the Gaudi is economical on fuel as well.

See how tedious this version is. Using pronouns helps to make writing more varied and less repetitive.

Personal pronouns

The most common type of pronoun we use is the personal pronoun. These are:

> I   you   she   he   it   we   they

Here are some examples:

> *I* like tea, but *you* prefer coffee. *He* likes lemonade, but *she* adores cola, although *it* is rather sweet. *We* all like orange juice, which pleases the parents, because *they* think *it* is good for us.

All the personal pronouns above are the subjects of their verbs (see pages 16 and 66). When these personal pronouns are the objects of their verbs (see page 68), then they change to:

> me   him   her   us   them

(*You* and *it* remain unchanged.)

Here are some examples where the personal pronouns are the objects of verbs:

> She's invited *me* to the party, but has she asked *you*? You haven't offended *her*. Not like Asim. She certainly hasn't invited *him*, but she likes *us*. As for the rest of our friends, I'm sure she hasn't ignored *them* either. Anyway, I'm going to enjoy *it*.

Starting point

Fill in the gaps in the following sentences with one of the personal pronouns (I, me, you, he, him, she, her, it, we, us, they, them).

a   I hate pasta but _____ love pizza.
b   See _____ on the big screen for the first time!
c   We told the police that we were being followed, but _____ wouldn't believe _____ .

d Do you like _____ as much as I like _____?

e Her mother told _____ to stop doing that, because _____ was irritating.

f Lovely, lovely oranges, buy _____ now!

Going further

1 There are errors in the use of pronouns in each of the following sentences. Find these errors and correct them.

a Between you and I, them haven't got a hope.

b Us went to the seaside, but she rained all day.

c I tried to tell they, but them wouldn't listen.

d Whatever your ambition, go for them!

e Me told he that the present was from I and you.

2 Read the following extract and decide where pronouns could replace nouns, leaving the meaning clear and making the writing much less repetitive.

> The day of the Grand Prix dawned. The day was rainy and the drivers were worried conditions would be dangerous. The drivers asked the organizers for a delay, but the organizers refused. Fortunately, the weather changed just before the start. The weather became warm and sunny, so the circuit dried out. The circuit was by then reasonably safe, so the drivers were pleased. The drivers felt safer in these driving conditions. The conditions were now similar to last year's.

Further still

In the article below, there are errors in the use of personal pronouns. There are also nouns which could be replaced by personal pronouns to make the article easier to read. Correct the errors and insert pronouns in place of nouns where appropriate.

SHEER GRIT AND DETERMINATION

The tournament was a triumph for the women's champion. Her regained the championship. The championship was won by sheer grit and determination. The champion's main competitors paid the champion full credit, saying that the champion deserved her win and that her win was proof of her courage. Her competitors clearly admire she, and me also think she is a worthy victor. Let we hope she returns next year.

Other Types of Pronoun

Possessive pronouns

The possessive pronouns are: *mine, ours, yours, hers, his, its, theirs*. They are used to show ownership.

Possessive pronouns stand in for nouns or they can stand on their own. They are not to be confused with the possessive adjectives, *my, our, your, her, their*, which are used with nouns to show ownership.

Note the difference between this pair of sentences:

I left *mine* in the classroom.　I left *my book* in the classroom.

Mine is the possessive pronoun and stands in for *my book*. *My* is the possessive adjective that tells us whose *book* it is.

Relative pronouns

The **relative pronouns** are: *who, whom, whose, which, that*. They refer back to something previously mentioned in a sentence and should be placed very close to the word they refer to.

He was the man *who* stood for the council.
I admired the painting, *which* had been painted in 1908.
They recognized the actress, *whom* they had seen in a play.
The trees *that* grew in the garden provided a lot of shade.
She's the woman *whose* lottery ticket was lost.

As these examples show, relative pronouns may be used to join one part of a sentence to another part. Along with conjunctions, relative pronouns are very important linking words in longer sentences.

Demonstrative pronouns

The **demonstrative pronouns** are: *this, that, these, those*. Again, as they are pronouns, they take the place of nouns or they can stand on their own:

This is no fluke!　*That's* the ticket!　*Those* were the days!

Demonstrative pronouns are not to be confused with demonstrative adjectives which always have to be attached to nouns.

That dog has fleas!　　　　　　　*Those* elephants look bored.

Other pronouns The words *who*, *whom*, *whose* and *which* may be used as **interrogative** (or questioning) **pronouns**:

> *Who* do you think you are?   *Which* of these do you dislike more?
>
> *Whose* is this?   To *whom* do we have to report?

The **reflexive pronouns** are: *myself, ourselves, yourself, yourselves, herself, himself, itself, themselves*. They emphasize the meaning of the noun or pronoun they relate to.

> He was very hard on *himself*.   They congratulated *themselves*.

Starting point

Read the following sentences. Choose the correct word from the selection given for each sentence.

a This is my/mine/mines and that is your/yours/your's.
b These/this book is great, but that/those one is boring.
c The discs are ours/our, but the CD player is their/theirs.
d Her/Hers is very neat but his/his's is untidy.

Going further

Fill in the gaps in the following sentences with one of these pronouns. Say what type of pronoun it is:

mine   ourselves   which   hers   that   whose   yours

a _____ of us is taller?
b _____ are these?
c We could have kicked _____ .
d I liked the one _____ came last.
e They preferred mine, but I liked _____ .
f _____ is the best choice.
g You shouted at the cat _____ was chasing the birds.

Further still

Fill in each of the gaps in the following letter with the appropriate pronoun and say which category each belongs to: personal, possessive, relative, demonstrative, interrogative, reflexive or other.

> Dear Claire,
> How have you been treating _____ ? _____ have
> been feeling very pleased with _____ since _____
> got the news about the exams. _____ proves _____
> am no fool, and anyone _____ says _____ am
> has been proved wrong. Between you and _____ , my
> parents have been pleasantly surprised by the news. A lot of
> the credit is _____ , of course, because _____ have
> always encouraged _____ . So soon I'll be at college near
> you _____ I hope will please _____ .
> Radhika

Conjunctions

A **conjunction** is a connecting or linking word used in the writing of sentences.

A conjunction can be used to connect words or phrases:

> Salt *and* pepper   Take it *or* leave it!

A conjunction is often used to join one part of a sentence (called a clause) to another part of the sentence (see unit on clauses, page 58):

> I was first in the queue, *because* I wanted a window seat.
>
> We were sad to hear that, *although* we had never liked him.
>
> You must stay until the train arrives, *as* I do not know her.

Relative pronouns and conjunctions are known collectively as **connectives**.

The main conjunctions

The most common conjunctions are:

> and   or   but

Other common conjunctions are:

> before   after   until   when   although   as   because   if
>
> in order that   nor   since   so   so that   than   that
>
> though   till   unless   whereas   while   whilst   yet

Conjunctions are essential when you are writing longer, complex sentences. Consider this series of short, simple sentences:

> I like cooking. Generally, I prefer creating more elaborate dishes. I can use my imagination. I can introduce special ingredients of my own choice.

The use of a succession of short sentences leads to repetition and a monotonous style, but by using conjunctions, four sentences can become one longer complex sentence:

> *Although* I like cooking, I generally prefer creating more elaborate dishes *because* I can use my imagination *and* can introduce special ingredients of my own choice.

Conjunction tips

Using conjunctions in your own writing

Aim to use a variety of sentence lengths in your own writing. At times it is appropriate to use short sentences if you want to state something directly. At other times, it is more appropriate to use longer sentences to explain or describe in greater detail. Sentence structure is discussed on pages 50–65, but note here that conjunctions are very often used to join subordinate clauses to a main clause, as in this example:

> I joined the company *in order* that I could travel, *because* I have always been fascinated by other cultures, *although* so far I have not managed to travel outside Europe.

Starting point

1 Pick out the conjunctions used in the following newspaper headlines:

a

WHEN WILL IT ALL END?

b

IF ONLY SOMEONE HAD TOLD HER!

c

WHILE THE CAT'S AWAY…

d

After the horse has bolted!

2 Gaps have been left in the following sentences, which you should fill with an appropriate conjunction.

a Time was running out, _____ I wanted to stay.

b Saquib left _____ Hayley came in.

c You could go for a walk _____ take a bus into town.

d I was surprised _____ she told me that _____ I had no idea.

e _____ we were late, we were allowed to enter, _____ we had a good excuse.

f _____ the game had ended, the coach congratulated the players, _____ they had lost.

g You have to prepare it _____ your guests arrive, _____ there will be no time later.

Going further

In each of the questions below, you are presented with a group of simple sentences. Link each group together to make one complex sentence by using conjunctions.

a I love swimming. It gives me the opportunity of healthy exercise. Swimming is not too energetic. I am also very good at it.

b Pets can be trained to be obedient. Pets can learn quickly. They should be treated with kindness and patience. Owners must reward them.

c It becomes very hot in this country. It is very close to the Equator. Average annual rainfall is not very high. The average rainfall is a major problem.

d The level of sales has decreased. People are worried about money. Unemployment has risen. There seem to be no prospects for improvement.

Further still

1 Below are more groups of simple sentences. Use conjunctions as connecting words to form one complex sentence from each group. Then for each new complex sentence, state two ways in which it is more effective than the simple sentences.

a Eating fruit and vegetables is essential for healthy living. Eating fruit and vegetables is a protection against disease. Fruit and vegetables are full of vital vitamins. They are also very tasty.

b How to manage your money should be taught in schools. Managing your money is an important life skill. People often get into severe financial difficulties. These difficulties could be avoided with a little forward planning.

Prepositions

A **preposition** comes before a noun or a pronoun and usually expresses something about its position, place or time in connection with other words in a sentence. Here are some examples:

> surging *through* the valley   shooting *between* the goalposts
> seated *behind* the table   ranked *above* the others
> starting *before* lunch   finishing *after* eight o'clock

The main prepositions

The most common prepositions are:

> above   after   across   against   along   among   around
> at   before   below   beneath   beside   between   beyond
> by   down   during   for   from   in   into   near   of
> off   on   onto   over   since   through   under
> underneath   until   up   with   without

The word preposition means 'to place in front of'. Think of a preposition as telling you something about the relationship between the word or pronoun that it comes in front of and the other words in a sentence. Look at these examples:

> The bridge stretched *across* the river.
> She said it was *beneath* her to visit him.
> The task was quite *beyond* us.

Prepositions of time or place

Prepositions usually tell us something about time or place:

> There was community singing *before* the Cup Final.

The word *before* in this sentence is a preposition of time because it tells us when the *community singing* took place.

> You will find your seats just *below* the gangway.

The word *below* in this sentence is a preposition of place, because it tells us where the *seats* are in relation to *the gangway*.

Prepositions as adverbs

When certain prepositions are attached to verbs, they alter the meaning of verbs and act as adverbs:

> I will *get by*, don't you worry.

In this sentence, *by* is attached to the verb *get* and alters its meaning to 'cope' or 'survive'.

In the next example, *by* is used not as an adverb, but as a preposition and makes no change to the verb *give*'s meaning:

> They were given their pay slips *by* the employer.

Starting point

1 Pick out the prepositions used in the following signs:

a
DON'T WALK ON
THE GRASS

b
NO PARKING BEYOND
THIS POINT

c
THE GATES WILL BE CLOSED
AT NINE O'CLOCK

d
KEEP TO
THE RIGHT

2 Fill the gaps that have been left in the following sentences with appropriate prepositions.

a The food was divided _____ the people.
b I would not turn up _____ four o'clock.
c He disappeared _____ the building.
d Our cottage is _____ that hill.
e The architect designed an ornate roof _____ the building.
f The apples fell _____ the tree.
g The athletes ran relentlessly _____ the track.

Going further

In the following report you are presented with a choice of prepositions. In each case, choose the correct preposition for the context.

> The leader of the party said she was beyond/beside herself with/at joy. They had won a victory before/beyond their expectations, a victory that until/beneath the very last moment they had not thought possible. On/In most people's opinions, the election was going to be a very close thing and the result would depend in/on/at a very few votes. Across/Against the odds, the party had won of/by sheer hard work. Now they had to think off/of the future and invest their energies underneath/in thinking up new policies. During/Along the campaign they had triumphed through their stamina, now they had to win through/between their ideas.

Further still

In the following article, some prepositions have been used as adverbs and some have been used as straightforward prepositions. Write down two headings: 'Prepositions as adverbs' and 'Straight prepositions' and list each usage of a preposition in the appropriate column.

> The threat of bullying will not simply go away. It would be easy to go over the top about this danger, but, on the other hand, the problem will not just blow over. It is something that many young people experience and this is a fact that society must face up to. Without crying wolf too often, the school authorities must come across some new ideas for fighting against this blight on the lives of so many youngsters.

Prefixes

A **prefix** is a syllable or a word which, when placed in front of a word, adds to or changes its meaning:

annual/*bi*-annual   national/*multi*-national   form/*de*form

Each prefix has a meaning or meanings of its own. For example, *bi-* means 'twice' or 'both', *multi-* means 'many', and *de-* means 'to make the opposite happen'.

There is no need to add or subtract a letter when you add a prefix to the stem of a word to alter its meaning:

satisfied/*dis*satisfied   ordinary/*extra*ordinary

necessary/*un*necessary   rate/*under*rate

The **stem** of a word is the basic form of the word without any additions for plurals and tenses or prefixes and suffixes. (For more on stems, see page 48.)

Sometimes a hyphen follows a prefix when two vowels meet:

de-ice   *by*-election   *pre*-arrange

Common prefixes and their meanings

1 **dis-** meaning 'the opposite of', 'fail to' or 'take away':
appear/*dis*appear   advantage/*dis*advantage   agree/*dis*agree
allow/*dis*allow   appoint/*dis*appoint   approve/*dis*approve
charge/*dis*charge   comfort/*dis*comfort   own/*dis*own

2 **mis-** meaning 'badly' or 'wrongly':
adventure/*mis*adventure   behave/*mis*behave
conduct/*mis*conduct   fit/*mis*fit   fortune/*mis*fortune

3 **sub-** meaning 'under', 'below' or 'subordinate to':
committee/*sub*committee   conscious/*sub*conscious
contract/*sub*contract   divide/*sub*divide   normal/*sub*normal
title/*sub*title   tropical/*sub*tropical

4 **un-** meaning 'not', or reversing some action:
able/*un*able   avoidable/*un*avoidable   aware/*un*aware
beaten/*un*beaten   biased/*un*biased   cover/*un*cover
conscious/*un*conscious   decided/*un*decided   lock/*un*lock

5 **under-** meaning 'below', 'lower', 'subordinate to' or 'insufficiently':
carriage/*under*carriage   coat/*under*coat   cover/*under*cover
ground/*under*ground   paid/*under*paid   value/*under*value

6 **re-** meaning 'again' or 'back again':
direct/*re*direct   appear/*re*appear   arrange/*re*arrange
assure/*re*assure   build/*re*build   call/*re*call

(For more on spelling and prefixes, see pages 116 and 118.)

Starting point

Here are some of the prefixes that are explained on page 38:

dis-   mis-   un-   de-   re-   sub-   under-

In the following list, the wrong prefix has been added to five words. Rewrite the words, adding the correct prefix to the stem word to give it real meaning.

disunderstanding   sub-connect   rerate   unconstruct   mis-divide

Going further

Here are some prefixes that are not considered on page 38:

> *extra-* meaning 'beyond what is usual' or 'outside of'
>
> *ex-* meaning 'out of' or 'former'
>
> *with-* meaning 'take away', 'keep back' or to 'put up with'
>
> *co-* meaning 'jointly', 'together'
>
> *in-* meaning 'not', 'lack of'
>
> *fore-* meaning 'at the front of', 'before'
>
> *pre-* meaning 'before' or 'beforehand'
>
> *super-* meaning 'above' or 'extremely'

a Using a dictionary, if it helps, write down at least two examples of words that have these prefixes.
b Explain in each case how adding the prefix changes the meaning of the original word.

Further still

In the following sentences, some words with a prefix have been left incomplete. Write down the completed words, making sure that they suit the meaning.

a He said he did not want to super- _____ his wishes about extra- _____ activities, but a pre- _____ of academic success was the ability to with- _____ pressure and not to mis- _____ your energies.

b Multi- _____ performers are not that common; some stars can act, but are under the mis- _____ they can also sing and dance, which is un- _____ for audiences who suffer the in- _____ of having to watch un- _____ performances while paying extra- _____ prices for seats.

c Sub- _____ temperatures brought mis- _____ to many homes; local authorities were accused of mis- _____ because they had mis- _____ arrangements for such un- _____ conditions and they had not fore- _____ the cold spell.

d The bi- _____ celebrations were under- _____ , which led to a dis- _____ lack of spectacular events.

Suffixes

Suffixes are single letters or groups of letters which, when added to the end of a word, form another word. For example: *disappoint* becomes *disappointment* with the addition of *-ment* and *imagine* becomes *imagination* with the addition of *-ation* (and the dropping of the final 'e').

Unlike prefixes, letters often are dropped or changed when a suffix is added. For adjectives ending in *-y*, for example, the use of the suffix *-ly* to form the adverb requires the original *-y* to change to *-i*:

happy/happ*ily*   cheery/cheer*ily*   funny/funn*ily*

Some common suffixes

When a suffix is added to a stem word, this can result in the word changing its class. Most of the examples below result in nouns changing to adjectives or in verbs changing to nouns.

1 **-ion:** accommodate/accommoda*tion*   confuse/confu*sion*
correct/correc*tion*   confess/confes*sion*   tense/ten*sion*
associate/associa*tion*   elect/elec*tion*

2 **-ous:** danger/danger*ous*   ridicule/ridicul*ous*   pomp/pomp*ous*
marvel/marvell*ous*   glamour/glamor*ous*

3 **-ious:** mystery/myster*ious*   grace/grac*ious*   caution/caut*ious*

4 **-eous:** courage/courag*eous*   advantage/advantag*eous*

5 **-able:** favour/favour*able*   honour/honour*able*
comfort/comfort*able*   remark/remark*able*   believe/believ*able*

6 **-ible:** sense/sens*ible*   response/respons*ible*   horror/horr*ible*

7 **-al:** magic/magic*al*   music/music*al*   practice/practic*al*

8 **-ally:** mechanic/mechanic*ally*   physical/physic*ally*
practical/practic*ally*

9 **-ful:** beauty/beauti*ful*   care/care*ful*   cheer/cheer*ful*
dread/dread*ful*   pain/pain*ful*   use/use*ful*

10 **-ment:** agree/agree*ment*   advertise/advertise*ment*
achieve/achieve*ment*   embarrass/embarrass*ment*

11 **-ance:** disappear/disappear*ance*   maintain/mainten*ance*

12 **-ence:** depend/depend*ence*   occur/occurr*ence*

13 **-ation:** examine/examin*ation*   discriminate/discrimin*ation*

14 **-ing:** run/runn*ing*   beg/begg*ing*   photograph/photograph*ing*

15 **-ive:** create/crea*tive*   sedate/seda*tive*

16 **-ly:** beautiful/beautiful*ly*   slow/slow*ly*   bitter/bitter*ly*

17 **-less:** care/care*less*   clue/clue*less*   hair/hair*less*

18 **-ed:** wish/wish*ed*   consult/consult*ed*   refuse/refus*ed*

(For more on spelling and suffixes, see page 120.)

Starting point

1 Add a suitable suffix to the following word stems to form a new word:

force_____   laugh_____   pity_____

manage_____   eat_____   accept_____

2 In the following article you are presented with alternative spellings of various words. Select the correct word for each choice you are given.

> Fashionible/Fashionable clothes are usually very expenseive/expensive. However, an occurrence/occurrance is happeneing/happening in the high-street shops that has produced amazment/amazement in the field of high fashion/fashtion. This revolushion/revolution may lead to the disappearence/disappearance of the industry as we know it. It marks a considerible/considerable achievment/achievement on the part of a few outstandingly/outstandingily talented designers.

Going further

Fill in the gaps in the following sentences by adding the correct suffix to the incomplete words.

a He argued forc_____ , but she stuck relent_____ to her viewpoint.

b I was summon_____ up the courage to act, when another opportunity accident_____ came my way.

c During the 1920s, America imposed a prohibit_____ on alcohol.

d The tenants reacted hostil_____ to the astonish_____ suggest_____ that rents were to be increas_____ without prior arrange_____ .

e The visitors were complete_____ overwhelmed by their humili_____ at the hands of an outstand_____ home team.

f At the instigat_____ of the local police, crime-watch schemes were establish_____ which logic_____ should have lead to an improve_____ in the figures.

Further still

a Add a suitable suffix (not -ed or -ing) to the following word stems or words to form another word.

b For each example, say which word class it starts in and which it becomes with the addition of the suffix, e.g. verb/noun or adjective/adverb.

approach   amend   basic   culture   boast   abbreviate
correspond   deregulate   distract   dominate   evacuate
general   heart   instant   invite   liquid   material   merit
motivate   outrage   permit   proportion   reduce   reluctant
riot   sceptic   segregate   style   thank   tradition

Person

There are three classes of person in speech and in writing: **first person**, **second person** and **third person**. This question of person relates to personal pronouns (*I*, *we*, *you*, *she*, *he*, *it*, *they*) or nouns and different forms of verbs (I *am*, you *are*, she *is*, they *are*).

Agreement with person

The subject of a sentence has a person: first, second or third:

> *We* sold the car too cheaply. (*We* – first person)
> *You* sold the car too cheaply. (*You* – second person)
> *He* sold the car too cheaply. (*He* – third person)
> *The woman* bought a car. (*woman* – third person)

Verbs are affected by the person of their subject. They change their form according to the person:

> I *wish* that I could go. (first)   She *wishes* that she could go. (third)
> They *wish* they could go. (third)

> I *go* to the cinema every week. (first)
> You *go* to the cinema every week. (second)
> He *goes* to the cinema every week. (third)

> We *have* no doubts. (first)   She *has* no doubts. (third)
> They *have* no doubts. (third)

> I *am having* a party. (first)   You *are having* a party. (second)
> He *is having* a party. (third)   They *are having* a party. (third)

(See page 16 for more on subject–verb agreement.)

Which person to write in?

You will have a choice of which person (first, second or third) you use in your own writing, particularly when you are writing fiction. This example contrasts two of these:

First-person narrative

> I had to wait for the next train. I did not know what to do, but I started wandering round the town. Little did I know that this would lead me into a great adventure.

Third-person narrative

> He had to wait for the next train. He did not know what to do, but he started wandering round the town. Little did he know that this would lead him into a great adventure.

First-person narrative sounds more personal, more immediate, because the first person of the narrative is telling the reader directly what happened to them. Third-person narrative is perhaps less personal, but it does allow the story-teller to describe events from the point of view of more than one character.

Starting point

1 Say which person (first, second or third) the following are written in.
a You too can be a winner!
b He's broken the record.
c We're over the moon.
d I'm as sick as a parrot.
e They're painting the town!
f The show starts at eight.
g The gang's all here.
h It's all or nothing.

2 Fill in the gaps in the following sentences with a pronoun of the appropriate person and say which person it is.
a _____ have found the accused guilty of the crime.
b _____ is finding it difficult.
c _____ want nothing for themselves.
d Because _____ are late again, _____ must stay behind.

Going further

There are many errors of person (subject) and verb agreement in the following diary entry. Pick these out and correct them.

MONDAY

I were very tired today because I were late in last night. The sale at Bannington's start today, but I has no money. All the family was meant to go to the play, but Mum am ill so we has to cancel. Generally, though, I feels good because I has been out a lot and the holiday have still a long time to run. The weather are cold, but that are to be expected.

Further still

a The following opening to a story is written in the first person. Rewrite it using the third person instead but using the same verb tenses as in the original.
b Then say how you think the narrative is changed by changing from first person to third person in this opening paragraph.

I look back into the past and I think about how things might have been. I have my regrets, but then regrets don't do you much good. At times, I think to myself, if only I had acted differently or if I had made different choices. For instance, on that day in my life when that golden opportunity presented itself to me. That day when all my hopes for my future seemed to open out in front of me. It started out as just another ordinary day in my life, but I was to find that an ordinary day can change into an extraordinary day before you know it.

Number: Singular and Plural

Most nouns have a singular and a plural form:

    table/tables   girl/girls   computer/computers

Although most nouns form their plural by adding -s to the singular form, others form their plurals in different ways, for example, by adding -es or -ies (dropping the final -y):

    stitch/stitches   penny/pennies

or by changing an 'a' to an 'e':

    man/men   woman/women

(See page 122 for more on the spelling of plurals.)

Countable and uncountable nouns

Some nouns are almost always only used in the singular form. Here are some examples:

    information   water   luggage   accommodation   weather

One way of thinking about it is to classify nouns as to whether they are **countable** or **uncountable**. A word such as *book* is clearly countable, because more than one book becomes *books*. However, *information* is uncountable because you cannot have two or more *informations*.

To become plural, uncountable nouns have to be attached to countable units in a noun phrase:

    Four pieces of information were given to each customer.
    Three glasses of water are required.

Much, many, little, few

The adjective **much** is used with nouns that are almost always singular and uncountable:

    Much time has been spent on this project.
    Much anger has been expressed about this plan.

Many is used only with plural countable nouns:

    There were *many victims* of the crash.
    Many trains were cancelled because of the strike.

Little and **a little**, like *much*, are used only with uncountable nouns:

    Little joy was to be had from that experience.
    I felt *little pride* in my achievement.
    I noticed *a little interest* in this new idea.

Few and **a few** are used only with countable nouns:

    Few buses ran that day because of the weather.
    There were precious *few reasons* why they should do it.
    A few holiday-makers trudged along the seafront.

Less and fewer

Less and fewer are two words that are often mistaken for one another. **Less** is used only with uncountable nouns and **fewer** only with countable ones:

Less money was available for grants this year.

Fewer men read novels than women.

Starting point

Say which of these nouns are countable (they are used in the plural form) and which are uncountable (they are almost always used only in the singular form).

thunder   beach   tiredness   laziness   tray   disc

intelligence   knowledge   sofa   chemistry   lounge

Going further

In the following sentences, you are presented with alternative words. Choose the correct word for the context.

a I did not have as much/many grievances as she did.
b Many/Much spectators agreed with her actions.
c I do not have as much/many money as he does.
d A few/A little information was given out about the crash.
e Little/Few hope was given of a rescue.
f Less/Fewer bargain-hunters came this time.
g Fewer/Less knowledge was needed for this examination.

Further still

Read the following passage in which there are many errors relating to number. Pick the errors out and correct them.

Comments

Editor's Picks

Driving for too long can lead to many exhaustion and much accidents. Drivers must get used to driving for less hours at a time and doing fewer mileage. A few more common sense and less dangerous ideas about driving as if in a Grand Prix could lead to much less accidents. Many debate has taken place over this issue, but little hard decisions have been made. Perhaps fewer attention should be paid to the needs of drivers, and more to the much potential victims of overtired drivers.

Comparatives and Superlatives

Adjectives and adverbs can form comparatives and superlatives, which are then used in comparisons. Look at these example sentences:

> She was the *stronger* of the two.
>
> He was the *strongest* of them all.

In the first sentence, *stronger* is the comparative of the adjective *strong*. The **comparative** is used to compare two people or things.

In the second sentence, *strongest* is the superlative of the adjective *strong*. The **superlative** is used to compare more than two things or people.

In the following examples, *further* is the comparative form of the adverb *far* and *furthest* is the superlative form of the same adverb.

> He lived *further* from the school.
>
> She lived *furthest* from the school.

Most adverbs, however, form their comparatives by putting *more* in front of them, and their superlatives by putting *most* in front of them:

> They behaved *more decently* than expected.
>
> We behaved *most decently* of all.

More decently is the comparative of the adverb *decently* and *most decently* is the superlative.

The comparative and superlative of adjectives

Most adjectives that consist of one syllable only (such as *strong*) form their comparative by adding *-er* and their superlative by adding *-est*:

> long/long*er*/long*est*   calm/calm*er*/calm*est*

Adjectives that end in *-y* usually drop the *-y* and add *-ier* or *-iest*:

> happy/happ*ier*/happ*iest*   angry/angr*ier*/angr*iest*

Adjectives with one syllable consisting of three letters and with a consonant at the end have to double the final letter before adding *-er* or *-est*:

> big/big*ger*/big*gest*   hot/hot*ter*/hot*test*

Adjectives that consist of two or more syllables generally form their comparative by putting *more* in front of them, and their superlatives by putting *most* in front of them:

> favourable/*more* favourable/*most* favourable
>
> beautiful/*more* beautiful/*most* beautiful
>
> relaxing/*more* relaxing/*most* relaxing

There are some irregular adjectives that do not follow any of these rules:

> much/more/most   many/more/most   good/better/best
>
> little/less/least   bad/worse/worst

The comparative and superlative of adverbs

Most adverbs form their comparatives by adding *more* and their superlatives by adding *most*, but adverbs that consist of only one syllable usually add *-er* for the comparative and *-est* for the superlative:

fast/fast*er*/fast*est*   hard/hard*er*/hard*est*

There are some irregular adverbs that do not follow any of these rules:

well/better/best   little/less/least   badly/worse/worst

Starting point

1 Write down the comparative and superlative forms of these adjectives:

keen   dark   reliable   mean   selfish   incredible   lucky

2 Write down the comparative and superlative forms of these adverbs:

slowly   fortunately   heavily   loudly   kindly

Going further

1 Fill in the gaps in the following sentences with an appropriate adjective either in the comparative or the superlative form, whichever is grammatically correct.
a I did my homework _____ than she did.
b Of all the books I read, that one was the _____ .
c Which of these two styles do you find _____ ?
d We trained for the match _____ than they did.
e Our presentation was the _____ of all the entrants.

2 Fill the gaps in the following sentences with an appropriate adverb either in the comparative or superlative form depending on the context.
a The accommodation was _____ than in the other resort.
b Of all the candidates, she argued her case _____ .
c Which of the two singers did you think sang _____ ?
d The train service ran _____ under the old management.
e The cheetah runs _____ of all the wild animals.

Further still

Read the following article and correct any errors in the use of comparative and superlative adjectives and adverbs.

The spokeswoman for the government stated that the situation was stabler now and littler crime was committed than before. However, more strong efforts to bring about peace had to be implemented and more good strategic plans had to be formed. They had been worrieder about the situation than more early, but the littlest improvement was best news. They were certainly happyer with the state of affairs and they would be reviewing matters rigrouslier from now on.

Word Formation

Every word has a **stem**: the basic form of a word to which can be added an **affix** (a *prefix* or a *suffix*) or other alterations for tense or number.

For example, the word stem *continue* can be added to in various ways to make other words:

> continuing   continues   continued   discontinue   continuation

Here is another example of a word stem and its variations:

> grace (*noun/verb*)   graceful (*adjective*)   gracefully (*adverb*)
>
> graced *(past tense of verb)*   disgrace (*noun*)
>
> disgraceful (*adjective*)   disgracefully (*adverb*)

All of these words stem from the basic form of the word *grace*.

Further examples of word stems

accept: acceptance (noun)   acceptable (adjective)   acceptably (adverb) unacceptable (adjective)   nonacceptance (noun)

belief: beliefs (plural)   believe (verb)   disbelieve (verb) disbelief (noun)   disbelieving (adjective)   unbelievable (adjective) unbelievably (adverb)

character: characteristic (adjective)   characterize (verb) uncharacteristic (adjective)   characteristically (adverb) uncharacteristically (adverb)   characteristics (plural noun)

define: definite (adjective)   defined (past tense verb)   definition (noun) indefinite (adjective)   indefinable (adjective)   indefinitely (adverb)

inform: information (noun)   informed (past tense verb) informative (adjective)   informatively (adverb)   informer (noun) misinform (verb)   misinformation (noun)

understand: understandable (adjective)   understandably (adverb) misunderstanding (noun)   misunderstandings (plural noun) understood (past tense verb)

Word building

The ability to recognize basic word stems and to add prefixes and suffixes to form other words is an important skill in extending your own vocabulary.

Ensure that you know the principal suffixes and prefixes (see pages 38, 40 and 116–121) and use them to broaden your range of vocabulary by developing word families as shown above.

Starting point   Pick out the word stems of the highlighted words in the following headlines.

The **Beginning** of a **Different Era**!

THIS **PERFORMANCE** WAS **UNBELIEVABLE**

The **voting** public say they are **disillusioned**

DOCTORS **CONCERNED** ABOUT CHILDREN'S **UNHEALTHY** DIET

Going further

1 Many word stems can be changed into nouns, adjectives and adverbs by adding a suffix. Change each of the following into a noun by adding a suffix and then write a sentence around each of the words you have formed to show how each word is used.
   a please
   b approve
   c sing
   d fund
   e preach

2 Change each of the following into a noun, an adjective and an adverb by adding a prefix and/or a suffix and then write a sentence around each of the words you have formed to show how each word is used.
   a interest
   b nerve
   c expert
   d appoint
   e appeal

Further still

Form words from the following word stems in the classes of words indicated.

a *appropriate*: a noun, an adverb
b *collaborate*: a noun, an adjective, an adverb
c *compete*: a noun, an adjective, an adverb
d *function*: an adjective, an adverb, another noun by adding a prefix
e *help*: another noun by adding a suffix, an adjective, an adverb
f *lead*: a verb by adding a prefix, an adjective by adding a prefix and a suffix, an adverb by adding a prefix and a suffix
g *mourn*: a noun, an adjective, an adverb
h *nation*: another noun by adding a suffix, an adjective, an adverb
i *peril*: a verb by adding a prefix, an adjective, an adverb

Simple Sentences

In speech and writing, the basic unit of meaning is a **sentence**. There are various different types of sentences. Being able to recognize these different types of sentences should help you in your own writing.

In a **simple sentence**:

- one idea is expressed, or one statement is made, or one question is asked, or one instruction is given
- there is one verb with a subject (see page 66)
- there is one main clause only (see page 56).

A simple sentence makes complete sense standing on its own.

Basic types of simple sentences

There are four main types of simple sentences. We will look at their basic structure, remembering that each type can be lengthened and expanded by adding other words or phrases, but not other clauses (if it is to remain a simple sentence).

Type 1: This simple sentence uses a part of the verb *to be* as its verb and there is a subject. Here are four sentences about fishing that belong to this type of simple sentence:

> They *were* excited about going fishing. The weather *had been* awful last time. However, the sun *was* out today. They *were* up very early.

Type 2: In this type of simple sentence, the subject does or did something, but the verb does not take an object. The verb is intransitive (see page 68). Here are four examples:

> The lion *roared* loudly. The birds *flew* off. The wildebeest *went* on the alert. The bush *reverberated* with the noise.

Type 3: In this type of simple sentence, the verb does take an object which means it is transitive (see page 68). The subject does something directly to the object. Here are four examples:

> The band *sang* their hit song enthusiastically. The fans *cheered* every line. They *applauded* them at the end. The band *acknowledged* this tribute to their talent.

Type 4: In this type of simple sentence, the subject 'appears' or 'seems' or 'feels' or 'looks like' or 'becomes'. Frequently, these verbs are followed by the verb *to be* and/or an adjective or adverb. Here are five examples:

> He *appears* to be quite well. He also *seems* in good spirits. He certainly *feels* optimistic. Things *look* good for him. He *is becoming* enthusiastic again.

Starting point

Fill in the gaps in the following simple sentences with one of these verbs:

ran   fired   shouted   seemed   crossed   delighted   became

a The winner _____ the finishing line.
b Her tennis coach _____ to be very pleased with her.
c The starter _____ the starting pistol.
d The commentator _____ into the microphone.
e I was _____ with the result.
f They _____ tired very rapidly.
g The runners _____ down the main street.

Going further

1 Read the following sentences and decide which type of simple sentence each belongs to: 1, 2, 3 or 4 (see basic types of simple sentences on page 50).

a The seagull squawked annoyingly.
b The audience were completely spellbound.
c There seems to be no case to answer.
d The decorator painted the kitchen.
e She seems to be quite calm about the whole thing.
f The athlete trained rigorously for the event.
g The teacher pressed the bell.

2 In the following extract, only some of the sentences are simple sentences. Pick these out and write them down.

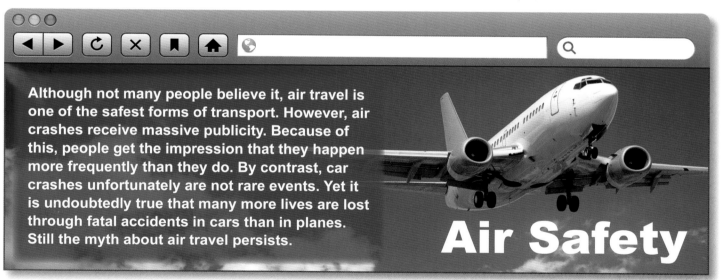

Although not many people believe it, air travel is one of the safest forms of transport. However, air crashes receive massive publicity. Because of this, people get the impression that they happen more frequently than they do. By contrast, car crashes unfortunately are not rare events. Yet it is undoubtedly true that many more lives are lost through fatal accidents in cars than in planes. Still the myth about air travel persists.

Air Safety

Further still

Fill in the gaps in the following passage with simple sentences of the type indicated.

> Theme parks are very popular with the general public. (type 2) _____ . There is a wide range of entertainments and activities available. (type 3) _____ . The popularity of theme parks has led to a vast increase in their numbers in the last ten years. (type 4) _____ .

Simple sentences may make a statement, issue an instruction, ask a question or express an exclamatory remark.

Statements and questions

The following simple sentences make **statements**:

> The exhibition was praised by the critics.
>
> She arrived at the station.
>
> At the bottom of the valley nestled a picturesque village.

Sentences can also be in the form of direct questions:

> What do you want?
>
> How deep is the ocean?

It is important to make a clear distinction between direct questions, such as the above, and indirect questions. **Direct questions** always have a question mark (?) at the end and, as the name implies, ask a direct question that requires an answer.

Indirect questions do not ask a question directly, but indicate that a question has been asked. Compare these examples:

> Have you done your homework?
>
> I asked him whether he had done his homework.

The first sentence is a simple sentence that asks a direct question. The second sentence is a complex sentence that asks an indirect question. Note that it does not require a question mark at the end.

Commands and exclamations

Commands (or imperatives) are instructions in the form of sentences. They may vary in tone, according to the context in which they are used.

> Mix the brown flour with the eggs.
>
> Clear the area, quickly!
>
> Take the first exit.

Note that the subject in imperative sentences does not actually appear, but is taken to be 'you'. Some commands require an exclamation mark at the end to emphasize urgency or strength of feeling.

Exclamations in the form of sentences express extreme feelings of joy, anger, sympathy, disgust, despair, etc. They can be recognized easily by the exclamation mark (!) at the end:

> What a wonderful life this is!
>
> I am absolutely disgusted!
>
> I simply can't believe it!

Using simple sentences

Simple sentences are used to express something very directly. A short simple sentence may be used to emphasize a point you are making or for dramatic effect, especially when it is surrounded by longer, more complex sentences.

In this paragraph, the short simple sentence is used to create a dramatic effect.

> The rush-hour crowds were intent on getting home because it was growing dark and rain was beginning to fall. *Suddenly, a strange piercing cry rang out.* People stopped in their tracks and looked round to see where this unearthly sound had come from.

Starting point

Make a note of whether each of the following is a statement, a question, a command or an exclamation.

a What do you think of the latest fashion?
b I rang the bell.
c Trees ringed the ground.
d Stand up!
e What a dreadful mess this all is!

Going further

1 Decide whether each of the following sentences is a direct or an indirect question, then add the appropriate punctuation mark at the end of each one: a full stop or a question mark.
a The instructor asked whether the driver had any questions
b What do I have to buy at the shop
c How am I expected to know the answer
d She wondered if I understood their software

2 The following sentences are in the form of direct questions. Turn them into indirect questions.
a 'Have you no money at all?' she asked.
b 'When are you due to arrive?' he demanded.
c 'How do you expect me to carry that home?' my mother asked me.

Further still

Read the following opening to a story. Gaps have been left, which should be filled with an appropriate sentence of the kind indicated.

'It's a beautiful day,' said Ankeet. '(command) _____ . I don't want to stay around the house. (exclamation) _____ !
(direct question) _____ ?'

'I don't want to get up yet,' replied Sean. (statement) _____.
(indirect question) _____ . (statement) _____ .'

'(exclamation) _____ ! I'm going to make the best of it.
(direct question) _____ ? (statement) _____ .'

Compound Sentences

A **compound sentence** consists of two or more simple sentences which are joined by the words *and*, *or* or *but*. Here is one example:

> 1 Cats are incredibly intuitive animals *and* have highly-developed senses of hearing and sight.

This sentence contains two verbs, *are* and *have*, but has one subject, *cats*, which is the subject of both the finite verbs. The two halves of the compound are joined by the conjunction *and*. The compound sentence in this particular example is used to make two points about the characteristics of cats.

Compound sentences are sometimes called **double sentences** or **co-ordinated sentences**. Here is another example of a compound or double sentence:

> 2 The forecast was for rain, *but* it turned out to be a very sunny day.

This time there are two different subjects: *forecast* and *it*. The two verbs are *was* and *turned*. The connecting word is *but* which balances the two halves of the sentence. Now look at this compound sentence:

> 3 You can cash in the vouchers *or* you can choose to hold on to them.

In this sentence, the subject of both verbs, *can cash* and *can choose*, is the same: it is *you*. However, unlike in sentence 1, the subject is repeated. The connective is *or*. This is the use of a compound sentence to state an alternative.

Multiple sentences

The examples of compound sentences we have looked at so far have all consisted of two 'equal halves', the combination of what are in effect two simple sentences joined by a connecting word. However, some sentences consist of three or more simple sentences joined by the conjunctions *and*, *or* or *but*. These are called **multiple sentences**.

> 1 Athletes have to be finely-tuned machines, *but* there is a danger of over-training *and* the more astute coaches are highly aware of this.

In this sentence, the three simple sentences within the multiple sentence are connected by the two conjunctions shown in italics.

> 2 Cars can be environmentally friendly *or* they can cause unpleasant pollution, *but* motor manufacturers have been made aware of their responsibilities *and* all new cars are now fitted with catalytic converters.

In this multiple sentence, there are four simple sentences joined by the three conjunctions shown in italics.

Compound sentence tips	**Too many compound sentences using 'and'**

It is best to avoid writing a succession of compound sentences using the same construction and joining words. Especially avoid writing a series of compound sentences that use *and* as the linking word:

I left the house about seven *and* walked to the station. I caught the bus *and* arrived at the cinema on time. We bought our tickets *and* went into the cinema.

The repetition of the same construction and the overuse of *and* creates a very monotonous style. It is better to use a variety of lengths and types of sentences in your own writing.

Starting point

Fill in the gaps in the following compound sentences with one of these three conjunctions:

and   or   but

a I could have had ice-cream _____ I could have chosen a pudding.
b The pitch seemed to be in good condition, _____ the innings got off to a bad start.
c The vet clipped the cat's claws _____ gave it an anti-flu injection.
d She intends to be a doctor _____ she might possibly become a dentist.
e The race was close, _____ the star athlete gradually drew clear.
f The bus was late _____ the passengers were angry.

Going further

Read the following groups of three or four simple sentences. Join together the sentences in each group into one multiple sentence using appropriate conjunctions.

a The plane approached the airport. The pilot was in contact with air-traffic control. The controllers were very concerned about landing it.
b The ice-dancer made some mistakes. The audience applauded her anyway. At least, they did not laugh at her.
c He was mad about computer games. His parents worried about this. They asked him to spend less time on the computer. They asked him to spend more time on his homework.

Further still

Read the following extract which consists of a number of simple sentences. Rewrite the extract in a mixture of compound and multiple sentences.

Soap operas are extremely popular programmes. Sports transmissions are beginning to rival them for audience figures. There are more women viewers for the soaps. More men watch sports. Both types of programmes have millions of viewers of both sexes. Young people also watch soaps. They are not necessarily the same soaps.

Complex Sentences

A **complex sentence** consists of one or more main clauses and one or more subordinate clauses (see page 58).

The **main clause**(s) in a complex sentence is the part that could make sense if it stood on its own without the rest of the sentence. The main (or principal clause) is the part of the sentence around which the rest of the sentence revolves and on which **subordinate clauses** depend.

Linking clauses in complex sentences

Unlike compound sentences which are joined by *and*, *or* or *but*, complex sentences may be joined by a whole variety of conjunctions. For example:

before   after   until   when   although   as   because   if
in order that   nor   provided that   since   so   so that   than
that   though   till   unless   whereas   while   whilst   yet

Here are some examples of complex sentences.

> 1 *The picnic has had to be cancelled*, since the weather is so bad.

In this sentence, the main clause, the part of the sentence that is really a simple sentence within a complex sentence, is in italics. It could make sense on its own. The rest of the sentence (*since the weather is so bad*) is dependent or subordinate to this main clause and is joined to the main clause by the conjunction *since*.

> 2 *The Grand Prix was marred by a fatal accident*, when the leading car, which was being driven by the world champion, spun off the track.

In this complex sentence, there are three clauses: the main clause of the sentence is in italics (or the part of the sentence that could make sense standing on its own) and two subordinate clauses. These two clauses (*when the leading car… spun off the track* and *which was being driven by the world champion*) are joined to the rest of the sentence by the use of the connectives *when* and *which*. Note that the second subordinate clause interrupts the first and is separated from it by commas.

Starting point

The following opening to a story consists of five sentences. Identify each of the sentences as belonging to one of three types of sentence: simple, compound or complex.

It was late-night shopping day in the centre of Ulford. Because it was so close to the holidays, the city was even more crowded than usual at this time of night. She stood alone in the middle of the bustling crowds and looked around her. Although she had made the decision to come to Ulford, she was wondering at that moment why she had done so. She was full of an awful sense of loneliness.

Going further

1 Identify the main clause in each sentence in the following extract from a speech.

> It is vital that people with disabilities have as many opportunities to play sport as able-bodied people. Although much progress has been made in recent years in raising awareness about the lack of suitable facilities, much remains to be done. It is as much about attitude as it is about money, although finance is an important factor, because local authorities complain about cuts in their budgets.

2 Identify one subordinate clause in each sentence in the following paragraph.

> The film was a huge box-office hit, although the critics had not liked it, which did not surprise the makers of the film. Because they had set out to make a very popular movie, the producers knew that it was hardly likely to win praise from reviewers who were looking for something more than entertainment value.

Further still

1 Below are groups of simple sentences from a student's presentation notes. Link each group of sentences together to make one complex sentence. Use conjunctions, relative pronouns, different kinds of clauses and correct punctuation.

a
> It is healthy to eat fruit and vegetables every day.
> Fruit and vegetables are full of vitamins.
> There are four main types of vitamins.
> All four are essential to good health.

b
> Hockey and ice-hockey are minority sports in this country.
> In America they are much more popular.
> There millions of people play and watch the sports.

2 Explain two ways in which the complex sentences you have made from these groups of simple sentences improve on them.

Subordinate Clauses

Complex sentences, then, are made up of different types of clauses, usually a main clause and a subordinate clause.

Clauses and phrases

A **clause** is different from a phrase because it has a subject and a verb.

> When *I get up* in the morning…

is a clause because it has a subject *I* and a verb *get up*. Whereas:

> in the morning

is a **phrase** because it is a group of connected words that acts in a sentence like an adjective, adverb or even a noun.

When I get up in the morning, however, does not make complete sense standing on its own. It needs a main clause in the sentence to complete the sense:

> When I get up in the morning, *I check my diary for the day*.

When I get up in the morning is a clause dependent on the main clause of the sentence, the section that could make sense on its own, *I check my diary for the day*. We call dependent clauses such as this **subordinate clauses**.

Subordinate noun clauses

Noun clauses are subordinate clauses within a complex sentence. As the name suggests, a **noun clause** takes on the function of a noun in a complex sentence. For example, the noun clauses within the following sentences are in italics:

> The tour guide announced *that there would be a slight delay*.
>
> *What could happen in the future* remains a puzzle.
>
> She asked *whether there was any possibility of a second chance*.

One useful way of recognizing a noun clause is to substitute the word 'something' for the whole clause and see whether the sentence still makes sense. Each of the above sentences makes sense when 'something' is substituted:

> The tour guide announced *something*.
>
> *Something* remains a puzzle.
>
> She asked *something*.

Connectives in noun clauses

The connectives *that*, *what*, *whether* and *why* are often used in noun clauses, as shown in the examples above. But it is quite usual to omit *that* in noun clauses:

> We announced we were going to leave the next day.
>
> The news agency reported the trial had ended.

Starting point

Write down the noun clauses in the following complex sentences.

a I asked what he intended to do.
b She said she had no plans to go on holiday.
c The Head announced there would be a half-day holiday.
d I did not know what he was talking about.
e What he meant became increasingly clear later.

Going further

The following sentences are longer complex sentences, in which there is more than one type of subordinate clause. Pick out the one noun clause in each of them.

a Although I had enough money, I did not want to pay such a high price and I asked whether I could get a reduced price ticket.
b What made me angry was the fact that I had thoroughly prepared for the meeting, which started very late.
c I argued that there was no problem about organizing the fête, which was always a highlight of the year, although it did entail a lot of work.
d Although communication by satellite was difficult, the astronauts announced their return to Earth, as they had successfully completed their mission.
e She queried whether there was any justification for their actions, which annoyed them because they believed so strongly in their cause.

Further still

1 Read the following newsletter and write down all the noun clauses that are used in it.

The club committee has decided fees will be increased from next month. The committee regrets that this action has had to be taken, but increased costs make it inevitable. It is hoped that members will understand the reasons for this action and that fees will be paid promptly. Members are to be asked whether they support plans to extend the premises, which have long been inadequate for the club's needs. The treasurer announced there were sufficient funds at this time to justify such an investment, which would be helped by the increase in membership fees. Some committee members, however, questioned what the benefits of such an extension would be.

2 Add one noun clause to each of the following main clauses.
a I asked her _____ .
b _____ puzzled the detective.
c The audience knew _____ .
d The quiz host announced _____ .
e _____ pleased the students.

Adjectival Clauses

Adjectival clauses have a subject and a verb. An **adjectival clause** describes a noun or a pronoun in a sentence:

> I like the group *who sang in the charity concert*.

The section in italics is an adjectival clause describing the group. The relative pronoun *who* joins the adjectival clause to the noun it describes.

> I chose this, *which came as a great surprise to everyone*.

The section in italics is another adjectival clause describing the demonstrative pronoun *this*. The relative pronoun *which* connects the adjectival clause to the pronoun it is describing.

The main relative pronouns which are used as connectives are:

> who   whom   whose   which   that

However, quite often the relative pronoun joining an adjectival clause to the rest of the sentence may be left out:

> Pistachio is the flavour most people prefer.

The 'full' version of that sentence would be:

> Pistachio is the flavour *which* (or *that*) most people prefer.

Other connectives may also introduce an adjectival clause:

> The plane landed *at* the exact spot where the previous one had.
>
> They arranged to meet at a time *when* it was mutually convenient.

Defining and non-defining adjectival clauses

There are two types of adjectival clause: **defining** and **non-defining**. Look at these two sentences:

> The horse *which was running for the first time* won the race.
>
> The horse, *which was running for the first time*, won the race.

The only difference between these two sentences is that the second adjectival clause is enclosed between commas and the first is not. However, this makes an important difference to the meaning. The first adjectival clause defines which horse is meant, i.e. 'Of all the horses in the race, it was the horse which was running its first race that won.' The second adjectival clause merely adds an additional piece of information about the horse. It is non-defining.

Starting point

Pick out the adjectival clauses in the following sentences.

a I just caught the bus, which was on time for once.

b The man, who was wearing a heavy overcoat, laughed outright.

c They bought comics instead of books, which did not please their aunt.

d The cats, whose owners were on holiday, were sent to the cattery.

e The horse that had jumped out of the stall ran last in the race.

Going further

1 Decide on an appropriate relative pronoun for each gap in the following sentences. In each case the pronoun should suit the adjectival clause which follows it.

a I had a very light meal, _____ was really tasty.
b Although I had the money, _____ was unusual, I was reluctant to pay.
c The student _____ essay had been lost was allowed to rewrite it.
d The teacher gave out notes, _____ proved very useful.
e The woman, _____ had waited a long time, entered the doctor's surgery.

2 Say whether each of these sentences contains a defining or a non-defining adjectival clause.

a The runners who were in the next race lined up at the start.
b The students, who were tired and disappointed, slumped down.
c Only those spectators who had come early were fortunate enough to get a good view.
d The players, who were very tired, trooped off the field with their heads bowed.

Further still

Read the following passage and identify all the adjectival clauses that are used in it.

The rush-hour crowds, who were eager to catch their trains and buses, streamed across the bridge, which was one of the busiest in the city. The fog that had threatened to settle all day finally closed in, which made visibility very difficult. The heavy traffic, which was clogging the streets, moved very slowly. The street lighting, which had come on early because of the fog, hardly lit up the scene, which, truthfully, was a depressing and dismal one. Some street musicians whose efforts the passers-by scarcely noticed were trying their best to lighten the gloomy scene. The city, which at times could look beautiful, was not at its best.

Adverbial Clauses

Adverbial clauses are subordinate to the main clause of a sentence and qualify the meaning of the verb in the main clause to which they are attached.

There are various types of adverbial clause: adverbial clauses of time, place, reason, manner, comparison or degree, purpose, result, condition and concession.

Adverbial clauses of time most commonly use these conjunctions: *when*, *as*, *as soon as*, *after*, *since*, *until* or *before*:

> *When we arrived at the station*, the train had already departed.

Adverbial clauses of place most commonly use the conjunctions *where* and *wherever*.

> I built the house *where the former building had stood*.

Adverbial clauses of reason use the conjunctions *because*, *as*, *since*, *whereas*, *for* or *why*.

> *Because I was worried about safety*, we cancelled the climb.

Adverbial clauses of manner use the conjunctions *how* and *as*.

> I designed the room exactly *how I preferred it*.
>
> I followed the instructions *as they had been written down*.

Adverbial clauses of comparison or degree are usually introduced by *than* or *as*.

> It was better *than I had expected*.
>
> She did not like the play *as much as I did*.

Adverbial clauses of purpose indicate the purpose of something and are usually introduced by *so that*, *that*, *in order that* or *in case*.

> I arranged it *so that I could attend the opening of the new shop*.
>
> *In order that the party would be a success*, a clown was hired to entertain.

Adverbial clauses of result are usually joined to the rest of a sentence by the connectives *so*, *so that* and *that*.

> The conditions were such *that the match had to be postponed*.
>
> *So that we can all get home early*, school will close at three.

Adverbial clauses of condition usually employ the conjunctions *if* and *unless* and explain the conditions under which something will, or will not, happen.

> The business will prosper, *if the sales forecasts are met*.
>
> *Unless you give a full explanation*, I cannot come to a decision.

Adverbial clauses of concession express something that is conceded or granted and they are usually linked by the connectives *though*, *although* or *even though*.

> *Although I played better after the break*, my opponent kept ahead.
>
> I enjoyed the outing, *though the weather could have been better*.

Starting point

Pick out the adverbial clauses in the following sentences.

a When I reached the cottage, it was dark.
b I will go wherever you want.
c Because of the bright light, she had to shade her eyes.
d I kept to the path, as I had been directed.

Going further

Each of the following sentences contains an adverbial clause. Pick these out and say to which type of adverbial clause each belongs.

a Although time was short, they looked round the shopping mall.
b Unless he gets his way, he becomes disgruntled.
c Their firm was much more successful than they had been last year.
d They sensed the danger so they took evasive action.
e They pitched their tents where they had previously.
f Before you depart, you must clean your room.
g If the restaurant is closed, we will have a takeaway meal.

Further still

The following notes on Abraham Lincoln are in three groups. Write three linked paragraphs, each based on one group of notes. Write in complex sentences. Avoid unnecessary repetition.

Group 1:
- Abraham Lincoln born 1809
- considered one of the great presidents of the United States
- American President 1861–1865
- became senator for Illinois: raised slavery issue
- elected President before outbreak of American Civil War

Group 2:
- two sides in American Civil War: the Union and the Confederacy
- Lincoln issued proclamation freeing slaves
- freeing slaves opposed by Confederacy
- Lincoln's famous Gettysburg Address: 'government of the people, by the people and for the people' statement

Group 3:
- re-elected 1864 towards end of Civil War
- just after victory for Union, Lincoln assassinated
- assassinated by John Wilkes Booth
- Lincoln's assassination shocked people on both sides of Civil War; helped to reconcile the two sides

Phrases

A **phrase** is a group of two or more words that do not form a sentence or a clause. A phrase can perform the same purpose in a sentence as a noun, an adjective or an adverb.

Noun phrases

Noun phrases do the same job in a sentence as a noun and the most important word in a noun phrase is, not surprisingly, a noun. All of the following are noun phrases:

> a scoop of ice-cream
>
> that enormous mountain
>
> second-hand goods of all kinds

Here each of these noun phrases is used in a sentence:

> How would you like *a scoop of ice-cream*?
>
> I want to climb *that enormous mountain*.
>
> The shop sold *second-hand goods of all kinds*.

Adjectival phrases

An **adjectival phrase** has the same purpose as an adjective in a sentence and the main word in the phrase is the adjective. The following are adjectival phrases:

> simply wonderful and relaxing
>
> foggy, cold and damp

Here each of these adjectival phrases is used in a sentence:

> Our holiday was *simply wonderful and relaxing*.
>
> The weather forecast says it's going to be *foggy, cold and damp*.

Adverbial phrases

Adverbial phrases do the same job in a sentence as an adverb and the most important word in the adverbial phrase is the adverb. All the following are adverbial phrases:

> rather surprisingly   very angrily
>
> more frankly   extremely quickly

Here each of these adverbial phrases is used in a sentence:

> *Rather surprisingly*, he called the whole thing off.
>
> She answered his question *very angrily*.
>
> I responded *more frankly* than usual.
>
> The car was being driven *extremely quickly*.

Prepositional phrases

A **prepositional phrase** contains a preposition which comes before a noun or a noun phrase. The following are prepositional phrases:

> behind the shed in the garden
>
> under the bright stars in the dark sky

Here each of these prepositional phrases is used in a sentence:

> The sunflowers are growing *behind the shed in the garden.*
> I sat dreamily *under the bright stars in the dark sky.*

Starting point

Decide which of the following are phrases and which are sentences.

a a marvellous, exciting and exhilarating show!
b It's terrifically hot.
c sad and lonely
d Speak clearly and slowly.
e in a month or two
f rather moodily

Going further

In the following sentences, say which type of phrase each of the italicized group of words is.

a *The immense ocean liner* sailed *quite majestically into the port.*
b *Over those mountains* there exists *a long-lost tribe*, who are *quite frankly much more civilized* than us.
c *Recent scientific research* has revealed *totally unexpectedly* that, *contrary to former evidence*, there is *a distinct possibility of alien life.*
d *The fast bowler* hurled *the new ball down the rain-soaked pitch at the terrified batsman.*
e *Under these circumstances*, the understanding and sympathetic judge dismissed *the list of charges against the accused.*

Further still

Fill in each of the gaps in the following film review with a phrase of the type indicated in brackets.

The latest science-fiction film is (noun phrase) _____
(prepositional phrase) _____ , so the producers are hoping
(adverbial phrase) _____ for a box office success in this country. The
film tells (noun phrase) _____ about the adventures of three people
(prepositional phrase) _____ . It has plenty of action and maintains
(adverbial phrase) _____ the pace and excitement throughout the plot.
The critics are divided (prepositional phrase) _____ , but most think
the performances of the stars are (adjectival phrase) _____ .

Subjects

The **subject** of a sentence or a clause is the person or thing (noun or pronoun) that the sentence or clause is about. A sentence has a verb and at least one subject. In main clauses, the subject usually carries out the action.

Subordinate clauses in complex sentences have to have a verb and a subject as well, but, unlike a main clause, they do not make sense on their own. They are dependent on the main clause for their meaning.

Subjects in simple and complex sentences

In these sentences the subjects have been highlighted in italics.

1 *He* reads his newspaper every day.
2 *I* was very happy because her *team* won.
3 *The students* were concerned at the high cost of living, *which* had risen steeply in the last academic year.
4 Even *you*, *who* don't like horror movies, will be interested in this film.

In sentence 1, *he* is the subject of the main clause and of the verb *reads*.

In sentence 2, *I* is the subject of the main clause and of the verb *was* and *team* is the subject of the clause which follows and of the verb *won*.

In sentence 3, *the students* is the subject of the main clause with the verb *were concerned* and the relative pronoun *which* (that refers back to the *cost of living*) is the subject of the clause with the verb *had risen*.

In sentence 4, *you* is the subject of the main clause and of the verb *will be interested* and *who* (that refers back to *you*) is the subject of the clause with the verb *don't like*.

Compound subjects

The subject and verb in a clause or a sentence must agree. This means that a singular subject must have a singular verb and a plural subject must have a plural verb.

When two subjects are linked by *and*, a sentence is said to have a **compound subject**:

> *Liam and I* have no doubts at all.

The compound subject, *Liam and I*, becomes a plural subject and requires a plural verb *have*.

> *The star and the rest of the cast* take a bow.

The compound subject, *the star and the rest of the cast*, (an individual and a group of people) has a plural verb *take*.

However, when you use *or*, *either/or* and *neither/nor* with subjects, then the subject is treated as singular:

> *Either* Brad Pitt *or* George Clooney is my favourite actor.
> *Neither* Asma *nor* Emma is coming to the party.

The verb *are coming* would be wrong here, because each subject is singular (*Asma/Emma*), as they are not joined by *and*.

(For more about subject–verb agreement, see page 16.)

Starting point

Write down the subjects of the following sentences. Are they singular or plural?

a The Chancellor is heading for battle with the city.
b The boys went down to the bus station.
c James and Louise are brother and sister.
d The teacher and her students went to the swimming pool.
e Sami or Amir has taken the book home with them.
f You are the only person in this position.

Going further

Identify the subjects of each clause in the following sentences:

a Ali went to the bank and Gina met him in a café afterwards.
b I went to bed early because my head was aching so much.
c Although Lei was disappointed about the defeat, she accepted it with good grace, which endeared her to her opponent.
d When the fox broke into the chicken coop, we were all really upset, even though we had done everything we could to protect it.

Further still

a Read this extract and note down all the subjects.

> My elderly relatives is arriving today. If their train are on time then they will be here by 4pm. Grandad will no doubt get off the train holding a newspaper: *The Times* are his favourite. Then he will come home and starts telling his terrible jokes. Usually, about fifty per cent of these is funny. I will just pretend to laugh as usual because Grandma and Grandad is generally good fun.

b Now check back over the extract and correct the errors in subject–verb agreements, particularly with compound subjects.

Objects

Direct objects

The **object** of a sentence (or a clause) is the person or thing that is acted upon by the verb. The subject carries out the action, the **direct object** is the object of that action:

> The player threw *the ball* into the net.

What happened to *the ball* in this sentence? *The player threw* it, so *the ball* is the direct object of the sentence.

> She thanked *Ben* profusely for his present.

What happened to *Ben* in this sentence? *She thanked* him, so *Ben* is the object of the thanking and is, therefore, the object of the sentence.

Just as there may be two or more subjects in a sentence or clause making up a compound subject, similarly, there may also be a **compound object**:

> The headmaster greeted *the parents and students* of the school.

The compound object of this sentence is *the parents and students*.

> I wanted to buy *some chairs, a table, two armchairs and a wardrobe.*

In this sentence, the compound object is *some chairs, a table, two armchairs and a wardrobe*.

Every sentence has to have a subject, but not every sentence has an object:

> The bells rang out over the valley.

In this sentence, the verb *rang out* does not act upon any object. It is called an **intransitive verb**. A **transitive verb** is one that takes a direct object.

Indirect objects

The **indirect object** of a sentence is affected by the action of the verb, but is not the person or thing that is directly acted upon:

> She paid *him* the money.

In this sentence it is *the money* that is acted upon and *him* that is affected by the payment of the money. That makes *him* the indirect object.

> The next morning, the club sold *fans* the tickets for the final.

What was sold? *The tickets* were sold, so that makes *tickets* the direct object of the sentence. To whom were the tickets sold? The tickets were sold to the *fans*, so that makes *fans* the indirect object of the sentence.

Very often the indirect object of a sentence can be recognized as it has a **preposition** in front of it:

> I did give it *to him*.

In this sentence, *it* is the direct object and *him* is the indirect object. However, you will have noticed that the preposition is often omitted:

> I gave *(to) him* the money.

Starting point

Pick out the objects in the following slogans.

a
DRINK A PINT OF MILK A DAY.

b
An apple a day keeps the doctor away.

c
BUY ONE TODAY!

d
Your country needs you!

Going further

Pick out the direct and the indirect objects in the following sentences.

a She addressed her remarks directly to him.
b The doctor told the parents the bad news.
c The waitress served her customers with the meal as usual.
d The winning team showed the other competitors no mercy.
e I had promised him the money, so I wrote him an official contract.
f This estate agent sold rich people very expensive houses.

Further still

1 Read the following article and pick out ten examples of direct objects.

Scientists who have been analysing the results of a series of experiments have congratulated themselves on their findings. Initial figures suggest good news and that the sponsors will be given good value for their investment. If the group follow precedents, they will begin a practical application of their findings within a few months and commercial companies may be marketing new products within a matter of two years. Scientists rarely count their chickens, but this research promises rich rewards. The leading members of the scientific team can also expect awards from scientific bodies.

2 Read the following opening to a story and pick out five examples of indirect objects.

I told him the bad news on a dark, sinister night in November. His housekeeper had just served us tea in the drawing-room. I handed him the note I had received a few hours previously. After reading it, he handed it back to me. 'This will cause trouble for quite a few people,' he said. 'Shall we tell the police the facts of the case?'

Active and Passive Forms

Active verbs

An **active verb** is a verb whose subject carries out the action of the sentence.

> 1 *The champion served* three aces in the match.

In the above sentence, the verb (*served*) is active, because its subject (*champion*) carries out the action.

> 2 *The team created* a detailed plan for the event.

Once again, the verb in the above sentence (*created*) is an active verb, because its subject (*the team*) carries out the action.

Passive verbs

In a sentence, when the subject has the action done to it, then the verb is described as **passive**.

> 3 *Three aces were served* by the champion in the match.

Look at sentence 1 above. Sentence 3 transforms the sentence by putting it into the passive. Instead of having the subject (*champion*) carrying out the action, the new subject (*aces*) has the action done to it.

The effect of this is a change of emphasis. In sentence 1, the emphasis is on *the champion*. In sentence 2, because the *three aces* is the subject, that is what is stressed.

Now look at sentence 2 above and see what happens when the verb is changed to the passive:

> 4 *A detailed plan was created* by the team for the event.

Once again, the emphasis shifts to the subject of sentence 4 (*plan*) and away from the source of the action (*the team*).

Active and passive verb tips

When to use passive verbs

Using active verbs in your own writing will make it more personal and direct, and less formal. For example, if you were writing a personal account of a holiday, it might be more appropriate to use active verbs than passive verbs. Look at these contrasting examples.

Writing actively:

> The next morning *we climbed* a small mountain. *We had* a lovely lunch on the lower slopes. Then *we made* a leisurely descent.

Writing passively:

> The next morning a small mountain *was climbed* by us. A lovely lunch *was had* on the lower slopes. Then a leisurely descent *was made* by us.

The effect here of writing in the passive is to make the writing seem less personal and direct when it needs to be lively and engaging.

However, for formal pieces of writing, when the style has to be objective and impersonal, passive verbs might well be appropriate. Take this report on a Science experiment:

Next the copper solution was heated by a Bunsen burner. The effect of this was measured and more chemicals were added.

Look out for the use of the passive to obscure the subject of a sentence in news reporting. Look at the difference in these two sentences:

The company caused the accident by a chemical leakage.
The accident was caused by a chemical leakage.

Starting point

Decide whether each of the verbs in the following sentences is active or passive.

a The golf ball was driven down the fairway.
b The train crashed into the buffers.
c The film was released nationwide at the beginning of the month.
d The managing director congratulated the staff on their work.
e The staff were congratulated on their work by the management.

Going further

Fill in the gaps in the following sentences with an active or passive verb, whichever is correct in the context. Indicate whether the verb you have used is active or passive.

a The plane _____ the signal to land.
b Asha _____ the violin in the orchestra.
c The experiment _____ by the chief scientist at the plant.
d In the ensuing confusion, the secret plans _____ by the spy.
e In the lush green field the sheep _____ contentedly.
f The lawn _____ by the gardener.

Further still

1 Read the following notes from a report and then change all the active verbs used into passive verbs, making any other necessary changes to aid clarity and avoid repetition.

2 Then explain briefly what effect the use of passive verbs has on the report.

Mr Giles observed the accident at a distance of 15 metres. He made a statement to the police. In it he described how the car that Mr Ladmore was driving mounted the pavement and struck a lamp-post. Another pedestrian, a Ms Browning, confirmed this account. The police also took a statement from the driver. He was not able to offer any cause for the accident occurring.

Phrasing in Sentences

Expanding sentences

Let us look at a very simple sentence:

> The cat sat on the mat.

The order of the words in this sentence follows this pattern: subject, verb, prepositional phrase. However, we can add other sections to the sentence in this way:

> *In the warm afternoon sun*, the cat sat *sleepily* on the *red* mat.

Now we have added a phrase at the beginning of the sentence, an adverb after the verb *sat* and then an adjective in front of *mat*.

We can also add subordinate clauses to expand the sentence further:

> In the warm afternoon sun, the cat, *which gloried in the name of Bud*, sat sleepily on the red mat, *which had been purchased only the day before.*

Now two adjectival clauses have been added: the first describing the *cat*, and the second describing the *mat*. The sentence, though lengthy, is clear and logical in its word order and in its **phrasing**.

Word order

The subject of a sentence need not necessarily be placed first, although, for clarity, you should not hold it back too long. The subject of the sentence below is in italics.

> During the long night, *the tourists* heard the wild animals prowling in the jungle.

Usually, words associated with one another should be placed next to, or close to, one another. For example, adverbs should generally be placed close to the verb or adjective they are qualifying:

> The survivors of the crash *clung desperately* to the life-raft.

However, the adverb in the above sentence could be placed as the first word of the sentence, if you wanted to stress the survivors' desperation:

> *Desperately*, the survivors of the crash clung to the life-raft.

Generally, whatever comes at the beginning of a sentence will be emphasized. Therefore, if you want to make an important point in a complex sentence, make it at the start.

> *The electorate voted against the government in overwhelming numbers*, because they were dissatisfied with its economic policies and because they felt like a change.

If you wanted to stress the reasons why the electorate took the action they did, you might consider this changed word order:

> *Because they were dissatisfied with its economic policies and they felt like a change*, the electorate voted against the government in overwhelming numbers.

Word order can affect the meaning of a sentence. So think carefully about the way you structure sentences, aiming to be clear, concise, logical and grammatically correct.

Starting point

Rearrange each of the following groups of words to create a grammatically correct sentence with the words in an appropriate order and with appropriate punctuation.

a slowly the gleaming white but surely rocket from the launch pad rose
b switched nothing else the bored to do with family on the television
c had spent could not buy I my money all I because anything
d the two left doorstep pints of happy-go-lucky milk milkman on the

Going further

The word order in the following sentences is either incorrect or clumsy. Rearrange the word order so that each sentence is clear, logical and well-phrased.

a The frequency was noted down of the trains by the agent secretly.
b Whose father was ill, she commiserated with her friend after a serious heart attack.
c The woman was rewarded, who had worked really hard, rather belatedly by the management with a free holiday.
d For the benefit of the poor, the rich man who left most of his money made a will late in life.
e Rising in the east, the onlookers watched the glorious sun, who had got up really early, and lightening the sky.

Further still

Rearrange the order of the clauses in the following sentences to give emphasis to a different part of each sentence. Then describe what effect this rearranging has on the meaning.

a As I had not agreed to this compromise, I refused to sign, which offended the others greatly.
b The journalist wrote her report carefully, because she wanted to be fair to both sides of the argument, which had by now reached serious proportions.
c Because they had suddenly been faced with a problem, which had puzzled many experimenters, the scientists began to think there was no solution.

Paragraphs

A **paragraph** is one section in a longer piece of writing. A paragraph usually consists of a number of sentences which deal with the same subject or one aspect of an overall topic. Read this paragraph:

> Part-time employment can be an important factor in the life of a young person. Not only can a Saturday or after-school job earn him or her extra cash, it can also give very useful experience in the world of work. The responsibility of taking on regular work teaches young people the need to be punctual and organized. However, there can be drawbacks and not all part-time work for students is satisfactory.
>
> One problem that can arise …

Notice how the paragraph is **indented** from the margin to give a clear indication of where it starts. This paragraph consists of four linked sentences. The whole paragraph deals with one topic: the issue of part-time work for young people.

Sentence 1 alerts the reader to what the main topic of the paragraph is. Sentence 2 puts forward the advantages that such work can bring. Sentence 3 follows on from this by mentioning specific things that can be learnt. Sentence 4 rounds off the paragraph with the point that there are some drawbacks, which leads naturally into the next paragraph.

Note that the new paragraph is again indented from the margin.

In your own writing, aim to write paragraphs that are correctly set out, deal with one aspect of the main topic and that consist of sentences which follow on logically from one another.

Block paragraphing

Block paragraphing is another way of setting out paragraphs on a page. With this layout, new paragraphs are signalled by leaving one line blank after the last paragraph, rather than by indenting from the margin. Thus, the paragraphs appear as 'blocks' on the page. This method is usually used in formal, business letters and in word-processed documents.

> Our records show that the invoice we sent to you on the 31st October last has not been settled. Another copy is enclosed.
>
> We would very much appreciate your settling this account as soon as possible. Like most businesses, we depend on customers paying their bills within a month.

Block paragraphing also appears in other types of continuous writing, such as reports and official letters. (For more on the setting out of letters, see page 106.)

Starting point

The following content has not been divided into paragraphs. Rewrite this webpage dividing it into three paragraphs.

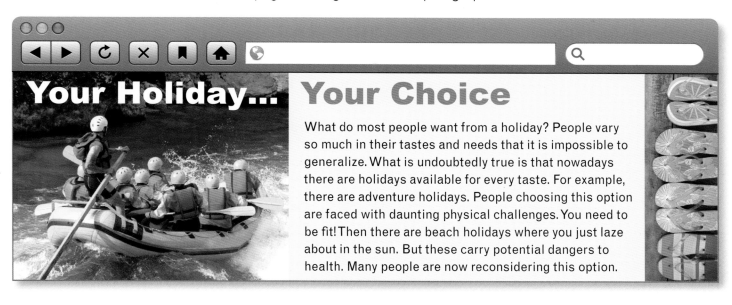

Your Holiday... Your Choice

What do most people want from a holiday? People vary so much in their tastes and needs that it is impossible to generalize. What is undoubtedly true is that nowadays there are holidays available for every taste. For example, there are adventure holidays. People choosing this option are faced with daunting physical challenges. You need to be fit! Then there are beach holidays where you just laze about in the sun. But these carry potential dangers to health. Many people are now reconsidering this option.

Going further

The following is the content of a formal letter. The writer is complaining about an item of clothing that they have bought online. Decide how and where to divide the content into three block paragraphs.

I regret that I have to return the enclosed item of clothing, which was sent to me recently. The order number for the garment is ORD/6543. My reason for returning it is that I am very dissatisfied with the quality of the garment. I read the relevant section of your website with great care and I had understood that the material would be high-grade cotton. I do not consider this is the case with this item. I have bought previous items from your website and this is the first time I have had to return anything. I would like a complete refund and I look forward to hearing from you about this matter.

Further still

1 Write at least three paragraphs on any one of the following topics. Each paragraph should consist of at least four sentences.
   a Summer
   b My Favourite Foods
   c Hobbies

2 Choose one of the topics given below and write a formal letter using a block paragraphing format.
   a A letter of complaint to the local bus company about a particular bus service
   b A letter to a charity organization asking for information to help you plan an event at school

Topic Sentences and Linking Paragraphs

Topic sentences

There are several ways in which a paragraph may be organized, but a useful approach is to think of the first sentence as being the **key** or **topic sentence**. This opening sentence will alert the reader to what the paragraph is going to be about. Consider this key or topic sentence as the opening to a paragraph:

> Basketball is a sport that is growing in popularity all over the world.

This topic sentence tells the reader that the paragraph is going to be about 'the growing popularity of basketball'. The sentence is not very long, and is concise and clear. It acts as kind of launch-pad for the rest of the paragraph. Sentences 2 and 3 follow on from it like this:

> Basketball is a sport that is growing in popularity all over the world. It has always been extremely popular in the United States where professional teams are watched by millions of fans. However, the game is now becoming 'big' in many other countries.

The topic of the paragraph has been expanded by these sentences. Now the closing sentence may round off the paragraph and perhaps introduce another aspect of the topic that might be continued in the next paragraph:

> Basketball is usually seen as a male sport, whereas netball is usually viewed as a sport dominated by women, although both sports are very similar.

Remember to follow this structure when planning any piece of continuous writing which has to be divided into paragraphs:

- Open with a key or topic sentence.
- Develop the point made in the topic sentence.
- Use a closing sentence that rounds off the paragraph and perhaps points the way to the next topic.

Linking between paragraphs

Paragraphs within a continuous piece of writing need to be linked together so that the complete text has continuity. There should be a logical development from paragraph to paragraph: one paragraph topic should flow on to the next paragraph topic.

To help with this, it is essential to use **linking words** or **phrases**. Here are some useful words and phrases that are used in this way:

> however   in addition   additionally   this   nevertheless
> firstly   secondly   by contrast   equally   another factor
> despite this fact   yet   similarly   as a result   consequently
> fortunately   unfortunately   therefore   thus   in conclusion
> lastly   finally

Starting point

Write a topic sentence for the opening of a paragraph on these topics:

a Computer Games
b Soap Operas
c Giving to Charity
d Keeping Pets
e Saturday Morning
f Winter Sports

Going further

Below are topic sentences that are the opening sentences of three paragraphs. Choose any *two* of them and develop the subject of each first sentence by adding a minimum of three linked sentences to form a coherent, structured paragraph.

a Homework is a necessary part of school life.
b Money is certainly not 'the root of all evil'.
c Girls and boys should have the same job opportunities.

Further still

Read the following notes which have been divided into three sections. Using these notes, write three linked paragraphs. Where appropriate, write in complex sentences using conjunctions and other connectives. Link the paragraphs together with linking words and phrases.

- rock and pop music industry big business
- generates incredible amount of money world-wide
- star performers make great deal of money
- record companies and concert promoters make great deal of money

- music industry not without its critics
- stories of performers being cheated out of earnings
- some unscrupulous producers and agents
- vast sums of money difficult to keep track of
- performers need good advice and protection

- constant care over accounts needed
- fans also can be cheated by inflated ticket prices
- fans often treated badly and have only distant view of their heroes
- interests of performers and fans should merge: fair deal for all

Formal and Informal English

Look at these extracts from two different letters.

Dear Sarfraz,

Great, wasn't it? What a game! I've never been as excited in all my life as when they scored that second goal. Brilliant! How can they follow that?

Dear Mr Home,

We regret we have to write to you about the recent invoice we sent you in relation to order no. 67543. Our records show that we still have not received payment, although the goods were dispatched to you on August 24th last.

The tone and purpose of each letter is quite different. This difference shows in the degree of formality in the writing and language chosen. The relationship between the writer and the receiver also has an effect on the tone and the language used.

The first letter is from one friend to another, so the tone and language are informal. The second letter is a business letter, where the writer (probably an employee of the company) is writing to someone they do not know personally (the customer).

Factors affecting formality of writing

These are the four factors that affect how formal any piece of writing should be.

- What is **the form** of the piece of writing? (e.g. personal letter, email, newspaper, magazine, formal essay, personal writing, official report)
- What is **the purpose** of the piece of writing? (e.g. to inform, persuade, entertain, enquire, complain, report, summarize)
- Who is **the audience** of the piece of writing – i.e. what is the relationship between the writer and the receiver or the reader? (e.g. close friend, business colleague, teacher, group or wide-scale readership)
- What is generally accepted as **the appropriate tone** for that particular form? (e.g. light-hearted tone for popular magazine article, serious tone for reporting of news in a 'serious' newspaper)

There are different degrees of formal and informal writing. For example, the following might be described as semi-formal:

> I would be delighted to accept your kind invitation to the opening of the new store next Tuesday.

Try to judge the appropriate tone and language for the form and purpose of each piece of writing you work on.

Starting point

Consider the following sentences and decide whether the language and the tone used are formal, semi-formal or informal.

a Go on, tell us another one!
b The bank and the building society are in merger talks.
c Cor! What a scorcher!
d The tension at Wimbledon has reached its peak.
e There has been a significant decrease in crime figures.

Going further

Read the following openings to letters and emails, and decide the degree of formality of each: is it informal, semi-formal or formal? Describe the audience for each letter and how this affects the tone and language.

a

Dear Sir,

Enclosed is this month's account statement.
I would bring to your urgent attention...

b

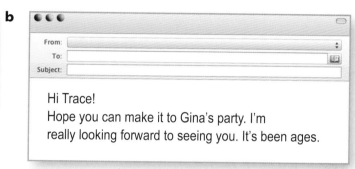

Hi Trace!
Hope you can make it to Gina's party. I'm
really looking forward to seeing you. It's been ages.

c

Dear Aunt Diane,
Thank you very much for the lovely
birthday present. I really appreciate it and
I look forward to reading it.

d

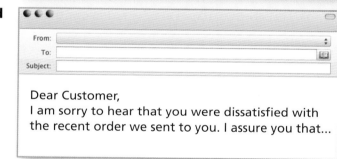

Dear Customer,
I am sorry to hear that you were dissatisfied with
the recent order we sent to you. I assure you that...

Further still

1 Write contrasting reports of the same news event as written by a tabloid newspaper and a serious, broadsheet newspaper. Choose an appropriate headline for each report and concentrate on getting the different tones right.

Then explain the differences between the two reports and your reasons for writing them as you have.

2 Imagine you are a DJ on a radio music programme. Write a short script for what you are going to say in the opening minutes, taking into account the type of radio programme it is and the average age of the listeners.

Then explain the factors that influenced your choice of tone and the language of the script.

3 Invent a script for a short news bulletin on a serious radio station. Consider the purpose and audience of the bulletin.

Then briefly explain how the purpose and context of the news bulletin affected your choice of tone and language.

Standard English and Dialects

Standard English is the way we describe the type of English that is used in most public written and spoken communication. The media (newspapers, magazines, radio and television stations) generally use Standard English to communicate with their audience. Most official communications (e.g. from the local council, from the government, from employers and businesses) employ Standard English. Indeed, Standard English is the most widely used dialect of English.

Most of us, however, are familiar with, and probably speak, a different dialect of English some of the time. Each **dialect of English** is spoken in a particular area or by a particular group of people. For example, dialects of English are spoken in different parts of Scotland, Wales, Ireland, England, and in Jamaica, Trinidad, different areas of Australia and the United States. These dialects all have their own different dialect words and grammar.

It is not the case that Standard English has correct grammar and that other dialects of English do not. It is rather that each dialect has a grammar that is appropriate to that particular dialect.

However, when so much communication uses Standard English, it is important to know how its grammar works.

What is appropriate?

Consider these two expressions:

> I leave m'yard early morning time.
> I leave hame affa early.

Both these statements are expressed in dialects of English: the first is in Jamaican English, the second in a Scottish dialect of English.

Both are correct according to the grammar of their particular dialect. If the communication is informal, for example in speech among friends sharing the same dialect or in an informal piece of writing, then it is entirely appropriate.

However, if you are writing or speaking in a more formal situation, where you may be communicating with people who do not speak your dialect of English, the Standard English version, *I leave home early in the morning*, is probably more effective.

The use of different or non-standard dialects of English in writing is often said to enliven it. In dialogue it can certainly help to bring characters and communities to life. However, this does not mean that Standard English needs to be dull and uninteresting. Whether you are using non-standard or Standard English, you should still have the same aim: to be clear, 'lively' and informative.

Starting point

Decide which of the following sentences are in Standard English and which are in another dialect of English.

a De sea is calm an' de sun is hot.

b Wouldn't it be luverly?

c I do like to be beside the sea.

d What's your gemme, eh?

e Sit down at your desks.

f Would you be after seeing that?

Going further

Consider the following situations for speech and writing. Decide, in each case, which it would be more appropriate to use: Standard English or a dialect of English that you are familiar with. Could you, in some of these situations, use either?

a A formal job interview in an area away from your own home
b A wedding invitation sent to relatives and friends
c A report on a scientific experiment
d A poem that describes some of the sights of your local area
e A fictional story told in the first person
f A written or oral examination in English

Further still

1 Choose any real or imaginary news story to write a report about. Write two versions of the report: one in Standard English and one in another dialect that you are familiar with.

2 Explain what differences you see in the two versions of your news report and any effect on the meaning that using these different types of English has had.

Improving Your Style

The style of your writing affects the meaning of what you write. Indeed, you could say that 'style is meaning', because it is almost impossible to separate the two. For this reason it is vital to try to improve your style in various ways.

Extending your vocabulary

Consider this sentence:

> The weather was *very nice* and the picnic was *very good*.

This is a grammatically correct compound sentence, but the vocabulary is very basic. Look at the difference that a change of vocabulary makes:

> The weather was *extremely sunny* and the picnic was *very enjoyable*.

This is better, but look at this third version:

> The weather was *extremely benevolent* and, as a result, the picnic was a *highly enjoyable event*.

Now the sentence has expanded and it is perhaps much more interesting to read.

It is tempting when writing to use familiar words, such as:

> nice   good   boring   marvellous   well

and sometimes they are entirely appropriate. However, your style and expression will be limited if you are restricted to very basic vocabulary. Reading a wide variety of fiction and non-fiction will bring you continually into contact with new words. Using a thesaurus is another way of extending your vocabulary. However, beware of using long, and seemingly impressive, words for the sake of it. This can have a negative effect on style and clarity.

Using a variety of sentence types

You can help to make your writing clearer by using a variety of types and lengths of sentences. Using a monotonous and repetitive sentence structure is a sign of a limited writing style. Read this short extract:

> We went to the park yesterday. Some of us played tennis. Others played mini-golf. It rained later on. We all went home for our tea. We had enjoyed ourselves.

The same sentence structure is used in all six sentences: subject plus verb plus object, prepositional phrase, adverb or pronoun. The result is a tedious and repetitive style. Consider this new version:

> When we went to the park yesterday, some of us played tennis and others played mini-golf. Although it rained later on and we all went home for our tea, we had enjoyed ourselves.

The six sentences have been changed to two complex sentences and the result is more 'flowing' and less repetitive.

Clarity and accuracy

Two important features of writing style are **clarity** and **accuracy**. These two features are closely linked. If a piece of writing is not clear, then it does not communicate effectively. If the accuracy of the writing is weak in terms of spelling, grammar and punctuation, then again communication is hindered.

Clarity can sometimes be impaired by using a rather pompous and unnecessarily long-winded style. Consider this sentence:

> As far as we can ascertain, the incidence of fatal accidents on this particular section of the motorway is in the region of five fatalities in the course of a year.

This second version is clearer because it is more concise.

> As far as we can tell, the number of fatal accidents on this section of the motorway causes around five deaths per year.

Starting point

Rewrite the following sentences replacing the words and phrases in italics with less familiar words.

a The meal was *very* nice, as the chef had *got* the various *bits* of the recipe *in just the right way*.

b The film was *good* and the cinema was *nice*, so a *good time was had by all*.

c The horse ran *well*, but the favourite *ran better*.

Going further

Rewrite the following sentences to improve on their monotonous and repetitive style.

a The gardener mowed the lawn. Then she cut the weeds. She then trimmed the hedge. After that, she took the garden rubbish to the dump.

b The beach was crowded. They found a clear section at last. They put up the wind break. They lay in the sun. They were careful about how long they stayed in the sun.

Further still

Choose one of the following events and write *two* versions of a report for a local newspaper. The first one should be long-winded and overwritten, using unnecessarily long words that impair clarity. The second version should be clearer and more concise without resorting to very basic vocabulary.

a School Sports Day

b The Opening of a New Hotel

c A Local Festival

Full Stops and Sentences

A sentence is the basic unit of meaning in any piece of writing. Sentences always begin with a capital letter. They usually end with a **full stop** (.), but they may also end with either a **question mark** (?) or an **exclamation mark** (!), where these are appropriate. (See page 90.)

Listening to the sense

It is important to be able to recognize when you have finished writing a complete sentence and when you should start a new sentence. To do this you need to listen to the sense of what you have written. You should 'hear' when you have finished saying one thing and are ready to start a new sentence to say something else. If you are in any doubt, read aloud what you have written. The 'sense' should tell you when you have completed a sentence.

Read the following short extract. Capital letters and full stops have been left out. Decide where they should be inserted by listening to the 'sense'. Speak the passage aloud, if it helps.

> The school bookshop will be open between 12.30 and 1.10 every Thursday a wide range of books is available to buy if you wish to order any particular title, please see Mr Jenkins you may leave a deposit on a book and pay the rest later students are asked to enter and leave the bookshop area quietly

If you read the extract aloud, you will probably have heard natural 'breaks', where one sentence has been completed and another should begin. This is what a correctly punctuated version would look like:

> The school bookshop will be open between 12.30 and 1.10 every Thursday. A wide range of books is available to buy. If you wish to order any particular title, please see Mr Jenkins. You may leave a deposit on a book and pay the rest later. Students are asked to enter and leave the bookshop area quietly.

So remember, always listen to the sense of what you have written. Ask yourself: 'Have I completed what I want to say in this sentence?' If the answer is 'Yes', mark that point with a full stop and start a new sentence with a capital letter.

Full stop tips

Incorrect commas instead of full stops

A common error is to use a comma instead of a full stop at the end of what should be a complete sentence. Sometimes lots of commas appear when full stops should be used:

> The sun rose golden in the sky, it was going to be a beautiful day, they woke early with the dawn, they felt very rested.

This is a bad case of someone inserting commas instead of full stops. There should be full stops after *sky*, *day* and *dawn*. Be careful not to fall into the same trap in your own writing.

Starting point

In each of the following short extracts, there are four sentences. Decide where the missing full stops should be by listening to the sense.

a The gerbil went missing the family were very anxious they looked all round the neighbourhood no one had seen him.

b The circus came to town there was a grand parade down the High Street the clowns capered among the crowd thousands watched.

c School reports will be sent to parents by 7 July if you do not receive your child's report, contact the school secretary the Headteacher asks for parents' cooperation over this matter it will be much appreciated.

Going further

Read this student book review and decide where the sentences should end. Rewrite the review inserting full stops and beginning new sentences with capital letters.

The latest book by Kate Alsop is a real winner although most of her fans are teenagers, I would not be surprised if some adults found this latest tale of hers intriguing it is a fast-paced adventure that starts off on a North Sea oil-rig and then moves on to Australia and New Zealand her many fans will certainly not be disappointed by her latest offering I will certainly be looking forward to her next

Further still

In the following extract from a travel book, some commas have been used at the end of sentences instead of full stops. Rewrite the passage replacing these commas with full stops and inserting capital letters where necessary.

Grand Canyon

The American West is full of staggeringly impressive vistas, the Grand Canyon is only one such natural wonder, vast mountain ranges contrast with endless valleys, these in turn give way to immense deserts where no human can safely venture, it is a country of amazing contrasts, its sheer scale is awe-inspiring, the courage of the early pioneers in crossing this continent cannot fail to impress.

Commas

Commas affect meaning

Inserting **commas** (,) or leaving them out can change the meaning of a statement considerably. Consider these two statements:

> 'Janet, my aunt is coming to stay,' he said.
>
> 'Janet, my aunt, is coming to stay,' he said.

In the first statement, the speaker is addressing Janet and informing her that his aunt is coming to stay. The comma after *Janet* tells us that this is the meaning.

In the second statement, the speaker is saying that his aunt's name is Janet and that she is coming to stay. The commas enclosing *my aunt* tell us that this is what is meant.

This is a clear illustration of how commas can dramatically affect meaning. It shows why you should be careful to insert commas to match the sense of what you have written.

Commas in lists

Commas are always used to separate items in a list:

> I need potatoes, cheese, minced lamb, aubergines and tomatoes.

Each item in this list has a comma after it except *aubergines* because that item is linked to the next item by *and*.

Sometimes a list of adjectives requires commas:

> The show was exciting, imaginative, moving and informative.

The insertion of commas follows the same rules as the punctuation of other lists: one after each item until the last two which are joined by *and*.

Be careful, however. Some adjectives go together, the first qualifying the meaning of the second:

> She wore a deep purple scarf to match her light mauve dress.

In such cases, separating commas would distort this meaning. Commas should also be used to separate a list of actions:

> The crowd at different times loved, hated or were indifferent to their team.

Commas and asides

Asides are brief phrases that add some non-essential information to a statement and are often used to emphasize a point:

> Speaking frankly, I think you're absolutely wrong.
>
> He has not, to my knowledge, been here today.

In the first example, a single comma separates the opening *Speaking frankly* from the rest of the sentence. In the second example, commas enclose the aside *to my knowledge* because it comes in the middle of the sentence.

Starting point

Insert commas in the following lists where you think they are necessary.

a He carried a bag full of oranges apples plums peaches melons nectarines and bananas.

b He felt weary angry frustrated and bored.

c Shall I wear my pale blue or my bright red jacket?

d The official read scrutinized leafed through and stamped my passport.

Going further

Fill the gaps in the following sentences with the suggested additions. Make sure you also use commas correctly.

a She was congratulated for her speech that was described as (four adjectives) _____ .

b (An aside) _____ there is no way of knowing whether the government will (three verbs) _____ .

c What I require for this particular recipe are (list of seven items) _____ .

d The students (an aside) _____ presented their views, which was very (three adjectives) _____ to the Head.

Further still

Read the following extract from a speech and insert commas where you think they are needed.

> To speak absolutely frankly I have no idea what to do. Any solution to this problem seems unlikely distant and inevitably controversial. People have argued canvassed opinion campaigned and demonstrated but the issue remains a frustrating complicated and possibly insoluble one. Ms Tench my immediate boss has to tell the truth worked immensely hard to bring a resolution that will be satisfying long-lasting fair and acceptable to all.

Commas to Mark Clauses

Commas very often have to be used to mark different clauses in a sentence. In a compound sentence (see page 54), a comma is frequently necessary to punctuate the two halves of the sentence, especially if the conjunction used is *but*:

> Australia won the match, but it was very close.
>
> African teams are packed with talent, but can one of them win the cup?

In complex sentences (see page 56), commas should normally be used to separate subordinate clauses from one another and from the main clause:

> Because the temperature had dropped to below freezing point, the pipes became frozen, which meant that a plumber had to be contacted.

Notice that a comma (after *point*) separates the first subordinate clause from the main clause of the sentence and another comma (after *frozen*) separates the subordinate clause that follows.

There is no need for a comma between *meant* and *that* because there follows a subordinate noun clause and usually that does not require to be marked by a comma.

Consider this further example:

> Although no reason was given, the early morning train was cancelled, which provoked resentment in regular travellers, who deserved better treatment.

A comma (after *given*) separates the first subordinate clause from the main clause, another comma (after *cancelled*) separates the main clause from the second subordinate clause and yet another comma (after *travellers*) separates the second subordinate clause from the third.

Adjectival clauses: defining and non-defining

Commas play an important role in the meaning of adjectival clauses (see page 60). Some adjectival clauses have to be enclosed within commas; others do not require commas because they define something about the people or things they are describing. Consider these examples:

> The group who were remaining behind were grateful for the rest.
>
> The group, who were remaining behind, were grateful for the rest.

In the first adjectival clause, *who were remaining behind* defines the group that is meant: it is one of a number of groups. The adjectival clause is a defining clause.

The second adjectival clause adds extra information about the whole group described. It does not pick out one group from among several. It is a non-defining clause. The commas clarify this fact.

Starting point

Insert commas in the following headlines where you think they are necessary.

a Nigeria Struggle But They Win!

b Rumours Fly But Government Deny

c When it's a Panther then you don't have to worry

d After pudding has been served which chocolates best round off the meal?

Going further

Insert commas in the following sentences where you think they are necessary.

a Because I had forgotten to bring a pen the teacher lent me one which I then forgot to return although she had reminded me to do so.

b They prepared thoroughly for the trek because they knew that the bush presented a demanding challenge which many other travellers had found difficult although to be exact not many had made such an attempt.

c Since the last visitor had left it was decided that the gates could be closed which made the staff much happier because they were extremely tired.

d As the decision had already been made the umpires strode onto the pitch which had dried out because the ground staff had worked so hard.

e He knew that something was wrong even though she denied it which did not surprise him as he suspected she was covering up.

Further still

Read the following report. Numerous commas have been omitted. Rewrite the passage inserting the missing commas where appropriate.

Only those students who studied French were allowed on the trip although many more wanted to go because the cost was low and they knew it would be well-organized because the French teacher had run it so often before. The selected students who were overjoyed to be going were given their detailed instructions. These ran to several pages because there were so many things to mention although the organizer had tried to keep red tape to a minimum. They would be staying in their twin town in the Loire valley and each student would be hosted by a local family.

The teacher who was planning the trip called the students together at the end of June. They would be leaving for France in two weeks' time which made it even better as they would miss the last week of term. They were told that as they would be representing the school abroad they would be expected to behave well at all times which came as no surprise to those who had been on trips like this before.

Question Marks and Exclamation Marks

Question marks

Question marks (**?**) are used to mark the end of sentences that ask a direct question. The following are all direct questions:

> What do you want for dessert?
>
> If there are no alternatives, what exactly do you expect us to do?
>
> Which route shall we take?

They are **direct questions** because the actual words of the question are stated. A direct question is something like direct speech where the actual words spoken are written down.

Indirect questions, however, do not use the exact words of a question and so do not require a question mark. Instead, the words of the question are reported, as in indirect speech. These are examples of indirect questions:

> The policeman was asked whether he had any clues.
>
> The passenger enquired whether there was an earlier train.
>
> We demand to know why prices have been increased.

(For more on different question types, see page 52.)

Exclamation marks

Exclamation marks (**!**) are used to mark the end of sentences which indicate a high degree of emotion, e.g. joy, fear, excitement, surprise:

> What a day this has been!
>
> I was never so surprised in my whole life!

Brief commands or instructions spoken in a curt manner are often followed by an exclamation mark:

> Turn that light out!
>
> Get out of here immediately!
>
> Be quiet!

Exclamation marks are also used after **interjections**, which are those phrases or single words that express strong emotion and stand alone in speech and writing:

> Oh no!   Ouch!   Marvellous!   Disgusting!   Phew!

Exclamation mark tips

Overdoing exclamation marks

There is a danger in overusing exclamation marks. They show strong feeling but if you overdo them, they lose effectiveness. In fact, they tend to dilute the emotions expressed. So use them sparingly and appropriately.

Starting point

Which type of question is each of the following sentences: a direct question or an indirect question? How can you tell?

a I asked her whether she wanted to come.
b What is the matter with you?
c I asked him what the matter was.

d I demanded to know whether he was going to honour his promise.
e How late do the trains run?

Going further

Which of the following do you think could justify the use of an exclamation mark? In each case, say why.

a Well, stone the crows
b I thought it was not at all believable
c Unbelievable
d That was stupendous

Further still

1 In the following extract, there are many examples of question marks that have been incorrectly used or omitted. Rewrite the passage correcting these errors.

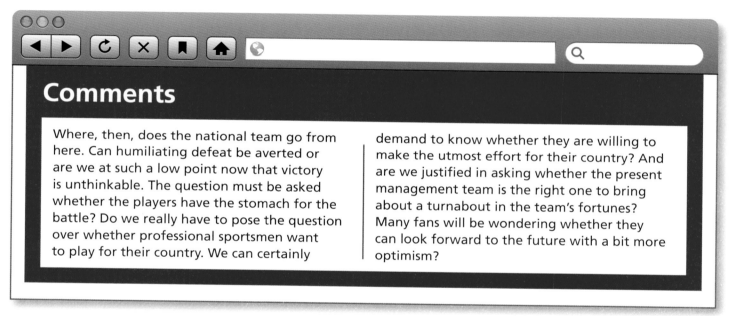

Comments

Where, then, does the national team go from here. Can humiliating defeat be averted or are we at such a low point now that victory is unthinkable. The question must be asked whether the players have the stomach for the battle? Do we really have to pose the question over whether professional sportsmen want to play for their country. We can certainly demand to know whether they are willing to make the utmost effort for their country? And are we justified in asking whether the present management team is the right one to bring about a turnabout in the team's fortunes? Many fans will be wondering whether they can look forward to the future with a bit more optimism?

2 The writer of the following postcard has used far too many exclamation marks. Decide which sentences or interjections need them and which do not.

Hi Helen!

I can hardly believe we made it to Spain! It's great! Amazing!
We've been to all the local beaches!
The sun hasn't stopped shining! And the food — it's fab!
Next time you really must come too!
We've missed you! So get saving!

See you soon!
Love, Sam

Semi-colons and Colons

Semi-colons for balance and contrast

A **semi-colon** (;) may be used instead of a full stop to separate two sentences that are very closely related to one another. Here is one such example:

> In Britain, the national sports are football and cricket; in Australia, they are cricket and rugby.

There are really two sentences in the above, but they are very closely linked together, and the use of a semi-colon indicates that. The second sentence follows on from the statement expressed in the first sentence.

Sometimes a semi-colon can be used appropriately when two linked sentences make contrasting statements:

> They love pasta; I can't stand it.
>
> I like the cinema; she prefers the theatre.

Semi-colons in lists

Semi-colons can also be useful in lists where the separate items run to several words:

> For this recipe I need the following: four free-range chicken breasts; several shallots; some sour cream or, if preferred, some natural yoghurt; two peeled apples and a few prunes; brown rice; a beaten egg and some flour.

The use of semi-colons in this long list helps to give clarity and emphasis to each item listed.

Colons before a list

A **colon** (:) is most commonly used when it precedes a list of some kind, as in the recipe example above. Here is another example of a colon being used in this way:

> Charles Dickens wrote a number of memorable novels: *David Copperfield*, *Great Expectations*, *Oliver Twist* and *Bleak House*.

The colon usually follows a statement that makes sense on its own and from which a list naturally follows, usually giving examples:

> There are three great enduring virtues: faith, hope and charity.
>
> The following were nominated for the award: Higgins, Hopkins and Healy.

Colons before quotations

Colons can be used to show that a quotation will follow:

> In Section B, para 2.5, you will find the following comment:
>
> 'A detailed analysis of the results must be undertaken.'
>
> She used the following quotation: 'This too shall pass.'

Starting point

1 Rewrite each of the following pairs of linked sentences, inserting a semi-colon where appropriate. Say whether they are balancing or contrasting sentences.

a My favourite colour is blue. Hers is red.

b In America, baseball and football reign supreme. In this country, it is football and tennis.

c The voters were in favour. The government, however, was opposed.

d Our friends love to cook for themselves. We prefer to eat out.

2 In the following sentences, a colon has been omitted. Rewrite each one, inserting the colon where it belongs.

a There are five continents Asia, Africa, the Americas, Europe and Australasia.

b Our last five games are against the following opposition Melbourne, Sydney, Adelaide, Perth and Tasmania.

c I nominate the following for membership Jen, Stu and Maggie.

Going further

1 Rewrite the following passage inserting semi-colons where appropriate.

> When I learned to read, it was picture books I loved, nowadays, it is novels that I like most. There are lots of reasons why I enjoy 'getting lost' in a good book: it helps me to relax, it enables me to see into the lives and minds of other people, it entertains me. There are so many good authors about at the moment we are really spoilt for choice. I can't wait for the next time I can escape into a book, in fact, it wouldn't be a true holiday without it.

2 In the following speech there are places where a colon should have been used. Rewrite the passage inserting colons where appropriate.

> There are three main issues that must be tackled unemployment, inflation and crime. We propose the following measures job creation, higher interest rates and a review of what causes serious crime.

Further still

Rewrite the following newsletter adding semi-colons and colons where appropriate.

Churley football club committee would like to propose the following new arrangements extended practice sessions on three evenings a week an indoor training régime for all team members tactical talks on the eve of matches the circulation of healthy eating guidelines. The aim of these measures are threefold increased fitness, contented players, success on the field.

Brackets, Hyphens and Dashes

Brackets

1 **Brackets ( )** are often placed around pieces of information that add to the information already being given:

> Then you add 50 grams (2 ounces) of sliced carrots.

In the above example, the information within the brackets explains what 50 grams are in ounces. Here is a further example:

> When you leave the M6, you take the Glasgow road (A74).

Brackets may also be used to give the dates of someone's life:

> William Shakespeare (1564–1616) was one of the greatest playwrights of all time.

Brackets may also be used for a reference that you want to draw to the attention of a reader:

> This topic is dealt with in chapter 4 (pages 45–57).

2 Often the information within brackets consists of a short phrase or a list that is explanatory:

> Tokyo (in Japan) is a very large city.

> Four of the largest countries in the EU (Germany, France, Great Britain and Italy) voted against the proposal.

3 Brackets may also be used to enclose an afterthought or comment on something that has just been expressed; the information within the brackets may not be absolutely essential to the meaning:

> She passed all her exams (that had been expected), but her grades were astonishingly high.

> We made our way to our seats (they had been reserved) and awaited the start of the concert in a state of great excitement.

Hyphens

Hyphens (-) are not used as often in English as they used to be, but there are still many occasions when the insertion of a hyphen changes the meaning of a word completely. Look at these contrasting headlines:

> **Manager Re-signs For Another Year!**   **Manager Resigns!**

With the hyphen, *re-signs* means the manager has signed another contract; without it, *resigns* means he has given up his job.

1 When two words are joined together to form a new word (**a compound word**) they are often hyphenated:

> panic-stricken   semi-detached   half-hearted   half-hour
> part-time   part-exchange   mother-in-law

2 A hyphen is often used when a prefix is added to a word:

> non-stick   co-opted   pre-school   co-author
> co-star   ex-Juventus   pro-Europe

However, the use of hyphens is becoming less standard and it is becoming more common for some words to do without a hyphen:

> coincidental   preamble   nonsense

Dashes

1 **Dashes** (–) may be used in pairs as an alternative to brackets when an explanation is involved:

> The whole team – the goalkeeper, the defence, the midfield and the strikers – played magnificently.

2 A single dash may also be used for this purpose when nothing else follows the explanation in a sentence:

> Plans have been made – plans that cannot be revealed at this stage.

Starting point

Use brackets in the following sentences where you think they are necessary.

a William Wallace 1272–1305 was a famous Scottish hero.
b The distance to the village is approximately five miles eight kilometres.
c This is mentioned elsewhere in this book chapter 8.

Going further

Rewrite the following passage, inserting hyphens where you think they are needed.

> Many parttime jobs are badly paid. Those people who are progovernment argue this is a nonissue, because unemployment figures are dropping. ExMPs, however, are critical of the statement that employers should cooperate with government in creating halfbaked schemes to solve this problem.

Further still

Rewrite the following passage inserting any brackets, hyphens or dashes that you think are necessary.

> Proanimal rights activists there are thousands up and down the country have been criticized for their antiscientific bias. Meg Harlow a spokesperson for a local group denies this charge and claims all medical research on animals is barbaric. When asked whether she is proviolence in the pursuit of the cause, she answered, 'There is a place for direct action direct action that remains peaceful in intent.'

Apostrophes to Show Omission

An **apostrophe** (') looks similar to a single inverted comma. It is used for two main purposes:

- in abbreviated words, to indicate that letters have been omitted
- in nouns, to indicate ownership.

Apostrophes to indicate missing letters

Consider the use of the apostrophe in these newspaper headlines:

It's a Girl!   That's the ticket!   Who's got the money then?

It's is the **contracted form** of *it is*: i.e. the two words are shortened and joined. The 'i' of *is* is missed out and the apostrophe indicates this.

That's is the contracted form of *that is*. Once again, the 'i' of *is* is omitted and the apostrophe indicates the missing letter.

Who's is the contracted form of *who has*. This time two letters have been omitted and the apostrophe indicates these missing letters.

Apostrophes in common contractions

Here are some examples of contractions involving a personal pronoun and part of the verb *to be*:

> *I'm* (I am)   *you're* (you are)   *he's* (he is)   *she's* (she is)
> *we're* (we are)   *they're* (they are)

Contracted forms also occur with proper nouns:

> *Priya's* gone away.   *Shannon's* got a summer job.

Here are some contractions of pronouns with *shall/will*, *have* and *had* where two letters have been omitted:

> *I'll* (I shall or I will)   *you'll* (you will)   *she'll* (she will)
> *we'll* (we will)   *I've* (I have)   *you've* (you have)
> *they've* (they have)   *you'd* (you had)   *he'd* (he had)
> *we'd* (we had)   *they'd* (they had)

Sometimes an apostrophe indicates where four letters have been omitted:

> *I'd* (I would)   *you'd* (you would)   *we'd* (we would)
> *she'd* (she would)   *they'd* (they would)

The apostrophe in negatives

When *not* is used to express a negative, contractions usually indicate the missing 'o' of the *not* by an apostrophe:

> *shouldn't* (should not)   *couldn't* (could not)   *isn't* (is not)
> *aren't* (are not)   *weren't* (were not)

But note these unusual exceptions:

> *cannot* in its shortened form is *can't*
>
> *shall not* in its contracted form is *shan't*
>
> *will not* in its contracted form is *won't*

Starting point

Rewrite the following sentences inserting an apostrophe where you think it is necessary.

a Its a beautiful day.
b Ill be going home tomorrow.
c Theyd love to come.
d Joes not here yet.
e I cant hear properly.

f Whos got the tickets?
g Wed have loved to have been there.
h I just wont do it.
i We shant refuse them.

Going further

Read the following email and insert apostrophes where necessary.

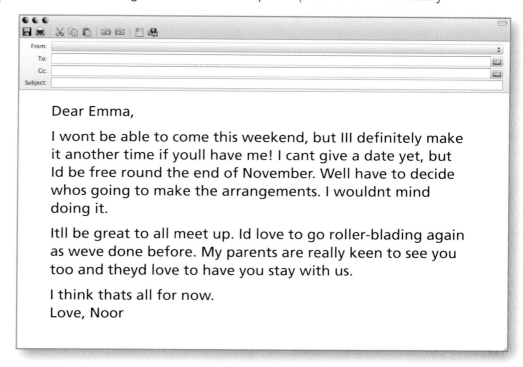

From:
To:
Cc:
Subject:

Dear Emma,

I wont be able to come this weekend, but Ill definitely make it another time if youll have me! I cant give a date yet, but Id be free round the end of November. Well have to decide whos going to make the arrangements. I wouldnt mind doing it.

Itll be great to all meet up. Id love to go roller-blading again as weve done before. My parents are really keen to see you too and theyd love to have you stay with us.

I think thats all for now.
Love, Noor

Further still

1 Make a list of song titles, or individual song lyrics, which contain contracted forms, e.g. *I'll Be There*.

2 Fill in the gaps in the following weather forecast with an appropriate contraction using an apostrophe.

_____ going to be an unsettled day tomorrow, so _____ better take an umbrella with you. _____ expect a few showers at least, and thunderstorms in some areas _____ be ruled out. _____ having it better on the Continent so if _____ headed for the south of France, then _____ probably be brilliant sunshine all the way. _____ no consolation for most of us, but _____ grown accustomed to uncertain weather this summer. I _____ forecast an immediate change for the better, but these clouds here, well, _____ likely to head off towards Scandinavia, bringing the prospect, _____ find, of some sunshine eventually later in the week. Well, _____ the weather. _____ have liked to have painted a more optimistic picture.

Apostrophes to Indicate Ownership

Apostrophes are also used to indicate ownership of nouns.

Apostrophes with singular and plural forms

Ownership of something singular is shown by adding an *s* to the noun with an apostrophe before it:

the cat*'s* paws   the animal*'s* jawbones

the car*'s* tyres   the government*'s* decisions   the woman*'s* hats

All these nouns are singular: there is only one of them and this is shown by the apostrophe coming before the *s*.

Look at what happens when these same nouns are plural:

the cats*'* paws   the animals*'* jawbones

the cars*'* tyres   the governments*'* decisions   the women*'s* hats

Except for the last example, the apostrophe is placed after the *s*, which shows it is the noun's plural form. However, *the women's hats* has retained the apostrophe before the *s* because *woman* forms an irregular plural (with no 's'): *women*. This is also the case with *man/men*, *child/children*.

As a general rule, singular nouns indicating ownership have an apostrophe before the *s* and plural nouns have the apostrophe after the *s*.

Nouns that end in '-s' or '-ss' follow the normal rule to ownership:

the abyss*'s* edge   the abscess*'s* growth   the countess*'s* dress

the dress*'s* hem   the dresses*'* hems

Some names end in 's' and when you want to indicate ownership, you can either put an apostrophe after the final *s* or you can add an *s* with an apostrophe before it:

Mr Jones*'* house or Mr Jones*'s* house

Dickens*'* novels or Dickens*'s* novels

Compound words

When compound words (two or more words joined by hyphen(s) to form one word) indicate ownership, the apostrophe comes in the final word of the compound.

the commander-in-chief*'s* orders   my son-in-laws*'* careers

Overdoing the apostrophe

Be careful not to be struck by 'apostrophitis', leading you to add unnecessary apostrophes to words. Remember that the possessive pronouns (*yours*, *ours*, *theirs*, *its*, for example) do **not** have apostrophes:

This is *yours*.   That's *ours*.   Those are *theirs*.   *Its* ball.

Another common error is to place an apostrophe in front of, or after, the final *s* when you are using a regular plural and no ownership is being indicated. If it is a straightforward plural and you are not indicating ownership, then there is no need for an apostrophe:

books   tables   sets   questions   diaries   discs   streets

It's and its   It is important to know the difference between these two words. *It's* is the abbreviated form of *it is* and so needs an apostrophe:

It's a lovely day today.   *It's* going to be a lovely summer.

Its is the possessive pronoun meaning 'belonging to it':

The cheetah lengthened *its* stride.

Its long legs worked like pistons.

Starting point

Insert an apostrophe in these headlines where you think it necessary.

a

The Countrys Triumph!

b

Mens Title Won by Newcomer

c

Farmers Complaints About Budget

d

Drivers Ability Questioned

Going further

Rewrite the following sentences correcting any wrong use of apostrophes and inserting any that are missing.

a The cat flinched and arched its back.

b The teachers assistant helped to display the childrens work.

c The mens voices were raised in anger at the officials refusal to see them.

d Its not clear whether their attempt's to break the world records' have succeeded or not.

Further still

Read the following passage from a play and rewrite it inserting apostrophes where necessary and correcting any incorrect use.

Waiter:	Our list of dessert's includes...
Boy:	How many ice-cream's have you got?
Waiter:	Its on the menu. Have you got your's, sir?
Boy:	What flavour's? I dont want just one flavour.
Waiter:	The menus beside you, sir. Can I take your order's?
Mother:	We must make up our mind's. The waiters waiting.
Boy:	I cant.
Mother:	Is there a special childrens menu?
Waiter:	No, its an all-inclusive menu weve put together for customer's convenience.
Boy:	Thats no good. I shant choose anything.

Direct speech is when the actual words someone has spoken are written down. It is different from **indirect** or **reported speech**. Indirect speech is when what someone has said is reported, but the actual words spoken are not written down (see page 104). Look at these examples:

> 'Our departure time will be delayed,' said the captain.

> The captain said that their departure would be delayed.

In the first sentence, the captain's speech is written down word for word. This direct speech is enclosed within **speech marks** (sometimes called inverted commas or quotation marks).

In the second sentence, the actual words the captain spoke are not written down, but reported. Therefore, no speech marks are necessary.

Punctuating direct speech

In punctuating direct speech, you have a choice between using single speech marks ('........') or double ("........"). Either is acceptable, but keep to whichever you choose throughout the piece of writing.

Read this short extract from a sci-fi novel and notice where the speech marks are placed. The numbered notes explain key points.

---

(1) 'We have to be on the look-out for meteors,' *(2)* said Commander Lock to his crew. *(3) (4)* 'Our meteor information centre has forecast a shower.' *(5)*

(6) 'Our meteor repelling shield will be operational within one-fifth of a second,' replied First Mate Batty, *(7) (8)* 'but I certainly hope it will not be necessary!' *(9)*

---

1 A speech mark indicates the opening of a piece of direct speech.
2 A comma is placed before the closing speech mark, marking the end of this stretch of direct speech.
3 A full stop rounds off after 'said Commander Lock...'
4 The Commander begins a new sentence, so a speech mark is placed before the first word which starts with a capital letter.
5 The direct speech ends and there is no 'he said', so a full stop is required inside the closing speech mark.
6 A new paragraph is required each time the speaker changes.
7 A comma is used as Batty is about to continue his sentence.
8 The speech mark opens again, but with no capital letter this time because no new sentence is begun.
9 There is an exclamation mark at the end of the sentence, inside the closing speech mark.

Starting point

Decide which of the following are examples of direct speech and which are indirect or reported speech.

a I told her that there was no alternative.
b 'Perhaps you've made a mistake,' he suggested.
c They demanded that they be compensated for their loss.
d The conductor replied, 'You must pay extra.'

Going further

Punctuation in the following short passages has been omitted. Rewrite each one punctuating it appropriately.

a the lawn has been mown I replied but the hedge needs to be trimmed
b the fans behaved themselves tonight the reporter said but what of the future will they behave when the tournament starts
c no she replied I will not cooperate I do not agree with the policy
d The cars are hurtling down the track the commentator shouted the champion is in the lead and no one can catch him
e I'm going home she said because I am cold and hungry you can do what you want
f Can we settle down now the teacher requested we are going to carry on with our set book please turn to page 34

Further still

Punctuate the following passage of direct speech.

I'm going to buy a motor bike said Juned.

Really? What make exactly? replied Jenny.

I'm not sure yet said Juned but I'm going to the showroom on Saturday to look around

Mind if I come along? said Jenny I like bikes

That would be great. I'm torn between a Japanese machine and a British one he continued which do you think

I'm not sure, to tell the truth Jenny replied I wish I had that choice

Why don't you save up and buy one? said Juned that's what I did

I will some day said Jenny when I pass my test

Then we won't see you for dust joked Juned.

You're right there, said Jenny I can't wait

Interruptions in Direct Speech

Paragraphing and interruptions

The main aim in setting out direct speech is to make it clear to the reader exactly who is speaking. One of the ways you do this is by starting a new paragraph each time a new speaker takes over. Here is a conversation between four different people:

> 'We must however, always be on the alert,' said the Commander.
>
> 'That goes without saying,' replied Batty, rather irritatedly.
>
> 'The Commander is right,' asserted Lyla, the First Mate.
>
> 'Meteors,' suggested Welsh, 'are a constant danger in this galaxy.'

The *he said, she replied* interruptions of the direct speech are another way of indicating who is speaking when there is a stretch of direct speech. It also helps to vary the type of interruption, as in the dialogue above. If every speech was followed by *he said* or *she said* it would become very monotonous. Thus, these alternative words are used: *replied, asserted, suggested*. Other possible variations are:

stressed   emphasized   commanded   told   ordered

mentioned   retorted   answered   questioned   enquired

asked   ventured   added   continued

Using variations like these can add an extra shade of meaning to 'interruptions'. However, beware of using too many different 'interruptions', as this can detract from the speech itself. Sometimes it can help the flow of the dialogue if one or two speeches are given no interruption at all, as this example shows:

> 'I love the circus,' she enthused.
>
> 'Do you?' he queried. 'Maybe circuses with no animals are all right.'
>
> 'Why do you say that?'
>
> 'There's no cruelty involved then.'
>
> 'Oh, I see what you mean.'

More about interrupted direct speech

Remember that when a speech in the form of a complete sentence is split by, for example, *she replied*, then it is a comma that is required after the *replied* and not a full stop. When the speech resumes, as it is part of the same sentence, no capital letter is needed:

> 'Does the Commander wish me to issue a special directive about this matter,' asked Batty, 'or will he do it himself?'
>
> 'The Commander will issue the directive himself,' replied the Commander stiffly, 'but he thanks Lieutenant Batty for his kind offer.'

Starting point

The following short sections of direct speech are correctly punctuated except for the lack of paragraphing. Rewrite the passages starting new paragraphs when appropriate.

a 'I've lost my purse,' wailed Harriet. 'Oh, no,' said Dan. 'Where did you have it last?' 'At the cinema last night.' 'Really?' said Dan.

b 'The team list is on the board,' said the captain. 'Is my name on it?' asked Jake. 'No, you're dropped,' joked Alistair. 'Don't listen to him,' said the captain. 'You're playing.'

c 'The lawn needs mowing,' said the wife. 'Yes, I know,' said her husband. 'Your turn, Dad,' said the daughter. 'Don't I know it!' Dad said.

Going further

Punctuate the following extract as direct speech, remembering to start new paragraphs when you think it is necessary.

the music festival should be allowed Tanita asserted because lots of young people love it but local people object to the noise replied the local councillor and last year lots of rubbish was left behind then make the organizers clear it up this year Conor suggested you could fine them if they didn't do it he added it's not enough the councillor answered the opposition to the festival is too strong but that's simply not fair moaned Tanita it's just about some older people trying to stop young people having some fun that's not the case replied the councillor

Further still

The following opening to a story includes direct speech between four different speakers. Rewrite the passage inserting punctuation and new paragraphs where you think it is necessary.

when did you detect the break-in the detective asked when I reported for work this morning the secretary replied I'm always first to arrive at nine Mr Porlock, my employer, usually comes in about ten minutes later do you know what's missing, Mr Porlock? the detective asked a considerable amount of money replied Mr Porlock there are also some documents some documents echoed the detective what documents some very important documents indeed Mr Porlock said emphatically what do you mean, Horace asked Mrs Porlock say what you mean yes, what particular documents the detective asked in a patient voice confidential documents replied Mr Porlock did you know about them, Ms Jethwa the detective asked the nervous-looking secretary naturally I'm privy to all the documents in the office responded Ms Jethwa but I'm not quite sure which documents Mr Porlock is referring to

Reported Speech

In **reported speech** (sometimes called **indirect speech**) the words someone speaks are 'reported'; the actual words spoken are not written down. Compare these two examples:

> 'My favourite fruit is bananas,' she said.
>
> She said that her favourite fruit was bananas.

In the first sentence, the actual words spoken are written down. This is direct speech (see page 100).

In the second sentence, the words spoken are reported. As the speech that is being reported happened in the past, the present tense of direct speech becomes past tense in reported speech. In this case, this means *my* becomes *her* and *is* becomes *was*.

Converting from direct to reported speech

When thinking about converting direct speech into reported speech, imagine yourself as a newspaper reporter. You overhear someone talking and you want to report what has been said to your readers. Of course, you could write down the actual words the person said, but there would be occasions when you would want to report what was said 'indirectly'. Consider the difference between these methods of 'reporting' in these two examples:

> 'I'm looking forward to working in Asia and starring in an Asian film,' said superstar Melanie Biffin yesterday at a press conference. 'The script for the movie is simply great and my co-star Brad Richmond is one of my favourite actors.'
>
> At a press conference yesterday, superstar Melanie Biffin said that she was looking forward to working in Asia and starring in an Asian film. She expressed the opinion that the script for the movie was great and that Brad Richmond, her co-star, was one of her favourite actors.

In the first version, the reporter has written down the actual words Melanie has said.

In the second version, the star's words are reported. This involves:

- changing the word order from the direct speech
- using the appropriate pronoun (*she* not *I*) and possessive adjective (*her* not *my*) where necessary
- linking the speaker with the words spoken using the word *that*, e.g. *she said that...*
- changing the present tense of the direct speech to the past tense of reported speech.

Remember, as the words spoken are in the past when they are reported, the **past tense** is the tense to use.

Starting point

Convert the following from direct speech into reported speech.

a 'What kind of sweets do you want?' Jamal asked Ella.
b 'I have a terrible cold today,' the teacher said to the class.
c 'The main picture is terrific,' he said, 'but the other one is awful.'
d 'I'd love to work with animals,' he said, 'because I respect them so much.'

Going further

The following passage is written in reported speech. Convert the reported speech into direct speech, making sure you punctuate it correctly and use paragraphing where appropriate.

> The courier said she wanted to point out some interesting tours holiday-makers could sign up for. There was a very interesting castle nearby and there were also some Roman baths, as well as an old monastery. There was a trip to a local restaurant where there would be authentic local dancing. One of the holiday-makers asked about the important matter of cost. The courier replied that all the tours were reasonably priced. Another holiday-maker asked whether they could pay for the tours by travellers' cheques. The courier assured them they could.

Further still

The following passage is an account of an interview in which direct speech is mostly used. Convert all the direct speech into reported speech and make other alterations as appropriate.

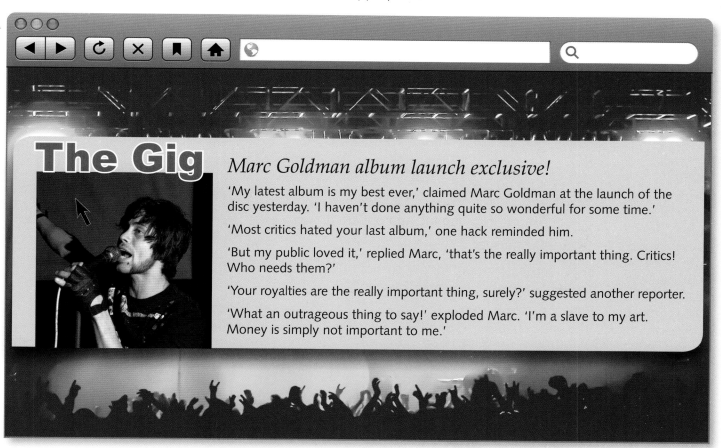

The Gig

Marc Goldman album launch exclusive!

'My latest album is my best ever,' claimed Marc Goldman at the launch of the disc yesterday. 'I haven't done anything quite so wonderful for some time.'

'Most critics hated your last album,' one hack reminded him.

'But my public loved it,' replied Marc, 'that's the really important thing. Critics! Who needs them?'

'Your royalties are the really important thing, surely?' suggested another reporter.

'What an outrageous thing to say!' exploded Marc. 'I'm a slave to my art. Money is simply not important to me.'

There are various conventions for the setting out and punctuation of letters. These differ between informal and formal letters.

An informal letter

Below is an example of an informal letter set out in the usual manner and punctuated appropriately:

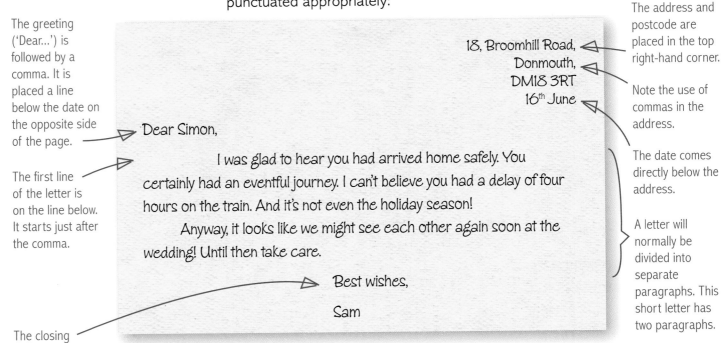

The greeting ('Dear...') is followed by a comma. It is placed a line below the date on the opposite side of the page.

The first line of the letter is on the line below. It starts just after the comma.

The address and postcode are placed in the top right-hand corner.

Note the use of commas in the address.

The date comes directly below the address.

A letter will normally be divided into separate paragraphs. This short letter has two paragraphs.

> 18, Broomhill Road,
> Donmouth,
> DM18 3RT
> 16th June

Dear Simon,

I was glad to hear you had arrived home safely. You certainly had an eventful journey. I can't believe you had a delay of four hours on the train. And it's not even the holiday season!

Anyway, it looks like we might see each other again soon at the wedding! Until then take care.

Best wishes,

Sam

The closing ('Best wishes' in this letter) is given a comma and is usually placed in the centre. Below that comes the writer's signature.

A more formal letter

For more formal letters, the layout for the sender's address and the date should follow the format above but the receiver's name and address should be added above the greeting. Look at this example:

The closing is usually 'Yours sincerely' if the receiver is named in the greeting, as he is here: 'Dear Mr Johnson'. 'Yours faithfully' is used if the greeting takes the more impersonal form: 'Dear Sir/Madam'.

Commas are inserted at the end of each line in the name and address of the receiver. A line is left before the greeting.

A comma is always placed after 'faithfully' and 'sincerely'.

C. H. Johnson,
Malone and Stack,
45 Hudson Lane,
Malchester
ML34 KI6

Dear Mr Johnson,

I am writing to apply for the post of office administrator as advertised in the *Nantburry Gazette* this week.

My current position with Grant & Co. in Malchester is similar to the one you describe and I feel I have the skills and experience to be considered for it.

Enclosed is a copy of my current CV for your perusal. I look forward to hearing from you in due course.

Yours sincerely,

E. Prowse

Starting point

Add the correct punctuation to the following extracts and make any necessary changes to the layout.

a

74 Agnew Lane Butterfield
BF12 3HH

Dear Joan I am so pleased to hear about your news.

b

I look forward to hearing from you soon.
Yours faithfully

George White

Going further

Read the following letter. Add any missing punctuation and correct any mistakes in layout, including the need for paragraphing.

25 Mildew Road
Aldington
AD13 5TY
17th May

Dear Sir
I am writing to apply for the position of storesperson that was advertised in the *Leader* last week. I am shortly to leave school and I hope to gain several exam passes. I have had a part-time job for the last year with Entwhistle and Son, a firm that deals in packaging materials. I think this job has given me valuable experience. I enclose some details about myself. I look forward to hearing from you.
Yours faithfully Daphne Brown

Further still

Rewrite this letter, inserting into the gaps indicated the words that are appropriate to a formal letter. Continue with a formal letter on a subject of your choice, closing the letter appropriately.

(Writer's address)
(Date)

(Receiver's name,
title and address)
Dear Madam

Key Vowel Combinations

Every word, however short, has to have at least one vowel. The **vowels** in the alphabet are: *a*, *e*, *i*, *o* and *u*. In some words, *y* is used as a substitute vowel for 'i':

> by   fry   cry   sty   my   why

To help you spell words correctly, it may help to say words aloud and to break words down into **syllables** (the separate sound units that make up the complete word). Doing this should make the spelling of individual words easier to recall.

Here are some examples of words broken down into their syllables:

> in/to (2 syllables)   mar/vell/ous (3 syllables)
>
> in/cred/i/ble (4 syllables)   dis/crim/in/at/ing (5 syllables)

Words with 'ea' and 'ee'

Every word, then, has at least one vowel, but some words have vowel combinations that produce a single sound. Take, for example, the combinations: 'ea' and 'ee', 'ei' and 'ie'. Words with 'ea' and 'ee' include:

> beads   defeat   feat   heater   meat   peat   real
>
> feet   meeting   peel   reel   seeing   seed   seem

The pronunciation of 'ea' and 'ee' is the same in all of the above. Words such as *feat*, as in: *It was an amazing feat to accomplish* and *feet*, as in: *My feet are very large* sound exactly the same, but the vowel combination is different. The same is true of *meat* and *meet*, *real* and *reel*.

How, then, can you remember which is the correct vowel combination for which word? First, try to see the whole word in your mind's eye and consider its meaning in the context in which it is being used. In addition, try to write the words down as often as possible. Add words with 'ea' and 'ee' that cause you difficulty to your own spelling list.

Words with 'ei' and 'ie'

One of the best known spelling rules in English is: 'i' before 'e' except after 'c'. This refers to occasions when the vowel combination 'ei' is pronounced 'e' as in *ceiling*. Words that follow this rule by having 'ie' and not 'ei' include:

> achieve   believe   niece   piece
>
> retrieve   tier   vie   wield   yield

The following words do have 'ei' after the 'c' because the vowel sound is 'e':

> ceiling   conceive   deceive   receipt

However, there are also many words that have the vowel combination 'ei' and do not follow the rule, including:

> beige   deign   feign   feint   geisha
>
> height   heir   heist   leisure   neighbour
>
> reign   seize   veil   weigh

Starting point

The following sentences offer a choice of spellings for some words. Rewrite each sentence, selecting the correct alternative.

a The reel/real truth is that we have achieved/acheived nothing.
b The hieght/height of the ceiling/cieling meant/ment that it beet/beat all but the tallest of us.
c The meating/meeting began on time, but the proposal was defeeted/defeated.
d The salad had peices/pieces of cucumber, sliced peaches/peeches, beatroot/beetroot and peeled/pealed potatoes.

Going further

Read aloud the following sentences and list the words that have incorrect vowel combinations in them.

a I have plenty of liesure time, but I still feal tired at the end of the day.
b My nieghbours are very noisy, which is a reel problem.
c He gave us his seel of approval, which we beleived was vital.

Further still

Read the following passage, picking out any spelling errors and correcting them.

My job was to retreive our position and not to yeild an inch to the competitor. I had to weild power, but I was not to vei with my team mates for glory. I was to fiegn confidence, even when the threat was at its hieght, and then I had to sieze the initiative. My acheivement would be known only by our most ardent supporters.

More Key Vowel Combinations

Words with 'ai' Some words with the 'ai' vowel combination include:

> afraid ailment aimless airborne brain chain
> claimant dairy nail paid painful remainder
> repair repaid said straight trainer trait
> vain waive

Words with 'au' Here are some examples of words with the 'au' combination:

> aubergine auction audience August
> aunt auspicious Australia authority
> automatic automobiles autumn cauliflower
> cause caution daughter daunting
> fault haunted jaunt laugh launch
> naughty nautical pause raucous
> sauce taut vault vaunt

Words with 'ia' Words with 'ia' combination include:

> amiable dial diamond phial diabetes diagnosis
> dialect dialogue diameter liable reliable viable

Words with 'ue' Words with 'ue', pronounced as a single sound, include:

> due guest rue rueful sue Tuesday

In some words, 'ue' is pronounced with two separate sounds:

> duel fuel

Words with 'ui' Words with 'ui', pronounced as a single sound, include:

> build building built guide guild
> guilt guilty guise guitar

Starting point

The following sentences offer a choice of spellings for some words. Rewrite each sentence, selecting the correct alternative each time.

a 'I'll have two place/plaice and chips,' said/sade Anna to the fareground/fairground employee.

b The comedian was very amiable/amaible and his jokes provoked a lot of laghter/laughter.

c As a general guideline/gideline, you should spend several hours a weak/week on manetenance/maintenance.

d The failure/fialure of the teem/team meant/ment that all their panestaking/painstaking preparation had been wasted.

Going further

Read aloud the following passage. Some of the words with certain vowel combinations have been correctly spelt, others are incorrect. Make a list of the incorrectly spelt words and correct them.

> I started keaping a dairy when I was much yuonger. When I told people at school, they thought I was vaugely odd becuase they said no-one kneads to write everything down these days. But the buisness of finding some time every day has been reelly good disipline for me. I now find that I have to biuld time into eech day to write down my thoughts and feelings and to include dailog from family and freinds. In the old days, it was an effort but now it has become an autamatic process.

Further still

Read the following diary entry. Some gaps have been left which you have to fill with one of the vowel combinations discussed in this unit.

JUNE 11

The rem_____nder of the exams concern me. But I have to ret____n

my cool and help my c_____se by forcing my br_____n to

tr_____n itself to absorb the necessary information. I'm looking

forward to _____gust and I know my hard work will be rep_____d

by having a great holiday then. I know I will not

_____tomatically pass the exams, but I am determined not to feel

g_____lty later on bec_____se I did not work hard enough. I must

b_____ld for my future. _____ntie Jean has asked me to be her

g_____st for a month in _____stralia in the _____tumn.

I feel rather n_____ghty, but I'm afr_____d of such a long j_____nt.

She's very am_____ble, of course, but I might call off under

the g_____se of previous engagements.

Spelling of Adverbs

An adverb is a word that qualifies the meaning of a verb, another adverb or an adjective by giving extra information about it:

> She ran *quickly* to the door.

The adverb *quickly* qualifies the meaning of the verb *ran*.

> It was an *exceptionally* beautiful day.

The adverb *exceptionally* qualifies the meaning of the adjective *beautiful*.

> We won the game *too easily* for our own good.

The adverb *too* qualifies the meaning of the adverb *easily*. These adverbs qualify the meaning of the verb *won*.

Adding -ly
Most adverbs are formed by adding *-ly* to an adjective:

> remote/remote*ly*   safe/safe*ly*   generous/generous*ly*
> proud/proud*ly*

Adjectives ending in '-al' still add *-ly* to form the adverb, giving an ending of *-ally*:

> exceptional/exception*ally*   rational/ration*ally*
> accidental/accident*ally*

Similarly, adjectives ending in '-ful' add *-ly*, giving an ending of *-fully*:

> careful/care*fully*   joyful/joy*fully*   successful/success*fully*

Exceptions to the rule
There are many exceptions to the *-ly* rule for forming adverbs. For example, adjectives ending in '-y' change the '-y' to *-i* before adding *-ly*:

> hungry/hungr*ily*   necessary/necessar*ily*   angry/angr*ily*
> happy/happ*ily*

Adjectives that end in '-ic' add *-ally* to form the adverb:

> basic/basic*ally*   frantic/frantic*ally*   sympathetic/sympathetic*ally*

Note, however, that there is one important exception to this rule:

> public/public*ly*

Words ending in '-le' simply drop the 'e' and add a *-y*:

> able/ably   capable/capably   dependable/dependably
> legible/legibly   probable/probably   terrible/terribly

It is worth remembering that there are no English words that have three 'l's one after the other. So words that end with '-ll' simply add *-y* to form the adverb:

> dull/dully   full/fully

There are three common adverbs that you should note the spelling of:

> duly (due)   truly (true)   wholly (whole)

Starting point

Form adverbs from the following adjectives:

> sad   crazy   lazy   immediate   reliable   realistic   resourceful
> public   dull   sarcastic   proud   pretty   beautiful   possible

Going further

In each of the following sentences, change the adjectives within brackets into correctly spelt adverbs.

a She joined in the game (enthusiastic) and found the whole experience to be (whole) invigorating.

b (Fortunate), we have (successful) completed the operation and we will (probable) be aiming to repeat it (annual).

c They had (extraordinary) good weather and they were (terrific) pleased about it.

d (Funny) enough, while you were (busy) engaged in doing that, I was (equal) involved in a (terrible) important task.

e (Basic), you have to write (legible), but if your work was (exceptional) good, they might (possible) make allowances for your writing.

f (Rational) speaking, there is no reason to doubt his story but, on the other hand, I have to listen to the other side (sympathetic) as well.

Further still

Read the following opening to a story and correct the many misspellings of adverbs in it.

Joe Baloney, private eye, was completly flummoxed. His partner, Fred Clueless, had mysteriously disappeared and Joe had duely been investigating the crime. He and his partner had occasionly fallen out, but Joe had taken his disappearance very personaly. Probabley, his partner had been ambushed by someone who knew him particularally well. There was definitly no suspicion that his wife had anything to do with it, principly because she was so tragicly cut up about her husband's disappearance. She had been sincerly shocked by the news.

Adding -*ing* and -*ed* to Verbs

Adding -*ing* to verbs ending in 'e'

When the continuous present, the continuous past or the present participle forms of the verb are used (*I am driving* or *I was driving* or *driving to work that day*), -*ing* has to be added to the basic form of the verb.

In cases where the verb ends in '-e', the '-e' is dropped and -*ing* is added:

> drive/driv*ing*   make/mak*ing*   forgive/forgiv*ing*
>
> lease/leas*ing*   judge/judg*ing*   measure/measur*ing*

The following examples show the -*ing* form of the verbs *escape*, *continue* and *struggle* being used in context:

> I *was escaping* from a tricky situation. (continuous past tense)
>
> *Continuing* down the path, I came to a large field. (present participle)
>
> She *is struggling* to meet her targets. (continuous present)

Verbs ending in a consonant

When -*ing* is added to a verb ending in a consonant, the consonant is usually doubled before adding the -*ing*:

> forget/forget*ting*   win/win*ning*   shop/shop*ping*   run/run*ning*

Remember, of the 26 letters in the alphabet, five are vowels (a, e, i, o, u) and the other 21 letters are **consonants**.

Adding -*ed*

Most verbs form their past tense by adding -*ed* to the basic verb form:

> address/address*ed*   accept/accept*ed*
>
> suggest/suggest*ed*   correct/correct*ed*

Verbs that end in a final '-e' simply add a -*d* to form their past tense:

> race/rac*ed*   surprise/surpris*ed*   assemble/assembl*ed*

However, when a verb with a single vowel (not a vowel combination) ends in a single consonant, it is usual to double that consonant before adding the -*ed*:

> grip/grip*ped*   plan/plan*ned*   chat/chat*ted*   fit/fit*ted*

Exceptions to this include verbs ending in '-er':

> suffer/suffer*ed*   loiter/loiter*ed*   stutter/stutter*ed*

Here are some more examples of verbs that double a consonant before adding the -*ed* ending:

> The audience clap*ped* loudly at the end of the performance.
>
> The scientist dip*ped* the iron into the solution.

Starting point

1 Practise forming the present participle of the following verbs by adding *-ing*:

draw obey enjoy pray pay bow know sow
allow vow

2 Form the present participle of the following verbs by adding *-ing* and making any other necessary changes to the verbs.

excite write like believe shake invite raise
blaze escape shine race

3 Correct any spelling errors in these newspaper headlines.

Rovers Loseing Out!   **Men Liveing on the Edge**   **We're All Smileing Now!**

Going further

1 Practise forming the present participle of the following verbs by adding *-ing* and making any other necessary changes to the verbs.

occur put stop plot travel bat beat skid
rid flit

2 Form the past tense of the following verbs by adding *-ed* and making any other necessary changes to the verbs.

struggle possess differ muddle report offend
kick refuse

3 Form the past tense of the following verbs by adding *-ed*. Make any other additions to the verbs that are appropriate.

plan prefer deter suffer regret concur slam
shovel revel

4 Correct any spelling errors in these newspaper headlines.

a   **The Same Mistakes Repeatted Again and Again**

b   **Finally They've All Rebeled!**

c   **Governments Argueing Among Themselves**

d   **Tax Evasion No Longer Permited**

Further still

Rewrite the following extract, correcting any spelling errors that you detect.

Traveling is one of my most favoured occupations. I have journeyd to many countries and I have been enthraled by most, but my recent trip to China exceedded my most exageratted expectations. My itinerary permited me to cross the country and I was staggerred by the variety of natural wonders this continent has been offerring to tourists for many years. I regreted that I had delayd a visit for so long. Why I had omited to do so was a mystery. My fellow tourists concured with that view.

Prefixes and their Spellings

A **prefix** is a syllable or a word which, when placed in front of a word, adds to or changes its meaning. The following words have prefixes:

> disappear   unhappy   foregone

The prefixes in these words are *dis-*, *un-*, and *fore-*. Each alters the meaning of the stem words: *appear*, *happy* and *gone*. (For more on prefixes and their meanings see page 38.)

Spellings and meanings

Knowing where the prefix ends and the stem word begins can help with the spelling of complex words. Understanding the meaning of the prefix can also be an aid to spelling the complete word.

For example, *de-* means 'away from', 'down' or 'to make the opposite happen'. Therefore, *deactivate* means 'to stop activating' and *decompose* means 'to stop being whole' (composed).

> The alarm system was *deactivated*.
>
> The food rapidly *decomposed*.

Other examples of words with the prefix *de-* include:

> debase   debility   decrease   decry   deduct   defame
>
> default   defect   defer   deficient   deflect   defuse

Here are some more prefixes and their meanings.

1 *a-* and *ab-* meaning 'of', 'from' or 'away':
   > ascribe   abdicate   abduct   aberrant   abnormality   absent

2 *circum-* meaning 'around':
   > circumference   circumlocution   circumscribe
   > circumspect   circumstance

3 *contra-* or *contro-* meaning 'against':
   > contradict   contraband   contraflow
   > contravene   controversy

4 *dis-* meaning 'not' or 'apart':
   > disability   disable   disadvantage   disadvantageous
   > disaffected   disagree   disappear   disappointment

5 *e-* or *ex-* meaning 'out of', and *extra-* meaning 'outside', 'beyond':
   > emanate   eradicate   excavate   exclusive   exclude
   > excursion   extracurricular   extraneous   extrasensory

6 *for-* meaning 'not' or 'apart':
   > forbid   forbear   forget   forgive

7 *fore-* meaning 'before':
   > forearm   foreboding   forecast   forefront   foregone
   > foreground   forename   foresee   foreshadow   foreword

8 *mis-* meaning 'wrongly' or 'not':

> misadventure   misapply   misapprehend   misunderstand
>
> misappropriate   misbehave   miscalculate   misconduct

9 *ob-* meaning 'in the way of':

> objection   obnoxious   obscurity   obsess   obsolete
>
> obstinate   obstruction   obtrude   obverse   obviate

10 *in-* (in this usage) meaning 'not':

> inactive   inaccuracy   inaudible   inadequate   incomparable

Starting point

Using a dictionary, find five words not listed on pages 116–117 which use these prefixes:

a *contra-* (meaning 'against')   **d** *in-* (meaning 'not')
b *dis-* (meaning 'not' or 'apart')   **e** *fore-* (meaning 'before')
c *ex-* (meaning 'out of')

Going further

Add an appropriate prefix from the list below to the incomplete words in the following sentences:

> fore-   ex-   dis-   contra-   de-   e-   mis-   circum-   extra-

a There is a total _____ diction in what you say.
b A _____ crepancy was discovered in the accounts.
c To be _____ warned is to be _____ armed.
d The club was highly _____ clusive.
e I cannot accept that he is a _____ interested party in the negotiations.
f Why should I _____ fer to your opinion?
g After _____ haustive questioning, the police decided to _____ liminate him from their enquiries.
h I considered their charges to be _____ orbitant.
i His reputation had fallen into _____ repute.
j You only have _____ stantial evidence for that judgement.
k Are you under the _____ apprehension that I like you?
l She almost certainly had _____ sensory powers.
m The driving instructor told her to _____ engage the clutch.
n It was a very minor _____ demeanour.

Further still

Here are five prefixes. Explain what each prefix means and then join each prefix to three stem words to make three new words.

a *circum-*
b *ab-*
c *ex-*
d *mis-*
e *ob-*

More Prefixes and their Spellings

Here are some further prefixes and their meanings. Knowing their spellings and meanings will help you in the spelling of complex words.

1 *inter-* means 'between', 'among' or 'together', when added to the front of a stem word. For example, *intercity* means 'between cities'.

> There was a regular *intercity* rail service.

Other examples:

> intercede   intercept   interchange   intercom
> interface   intermittent

2 *intro-* is another prefix meaning 'in', 'into' or 'inward'. For example, *introduce* means 'bring in' or 'present':

> I *introduced* my friends to my parents.

Other examples:

> introductory   introspection   introvert

3 *pre-* and *post-* are prefixes that denote time: 'before' (*pre-*), 'after' (*post-*). For example, *predict* means 'foresee' and *postscript* is something added after a piece of writing.

> I never *predict* the results of matches.
> She added an interesting *postscript* to her letter.

Other examples using the prefix *pre-*:

> precede   preconceive   precondition   prejudge   prelude
> premature   prescribe   presume   presuppose   prevent

Other examples using the prefix *post-*:

> post-date   postpaid   postgraduate   post-haste
> post-mortem   post-natal

4 *sub-* meaning 'under' and *super-* meaning 'above' or 'beyond':

> We are entirely *subservient* to the rules of the association.
> He made *superhuman* efforts to win the race.

Other examples using the prefix *sub-*:

> subconscious   subhuman   subjective   subjugate   sublet
> submit   subnormal   subordinate   subscribe

Other examples using the prefix *super-*:

> supercilious   superficial   superfluous   supermarket
> superhero   superimpose   superintendent   superiority
> superstitious

Prefix spelling tips   Adding or taking away?

There is no need to add an extra letter (or subtract a letter) when joining a prefix to a word. Here are some examples:

> disappointment not *diss*appointment
> forbidden not *fore*bidden

Starting point

Use a dictionary to find words using the following prefixes that do not appear in any of the examples mentioned on page 118:

a *inter-* (meaning 'between')
b *intro-* (meaning 'in' or 'inward')
c *pre-* (meaning 'before')
d *post-* (meaning 'after')
e *sub-* (meaning 'under')

Going further

1 Gaps have been left in some words with prefixes in the following sentences. Decide on the appropriate prefix to fill each space.

a A _____ condition of his accepting was that I _____ date the cheque.

b I considered her to be very _____ cilious in her manner when she said that I was nothing but _____ stitious.

c It was only my _____ jective judgement, but I thought he was _____ versive in his opinions.

d You will have to _____ tract a _____ stantial amount from the _____ total.

e I do not wish to _____ impose my own ideas, but these suggestions offer _____ lative opportunities.

f The detective _____ sumed that his _____ vention would be a success.

g It would be wrong to _____ judge the case and assume the crime was _____ meditated.

h Although the rain was only _____ mittent, the efforts of the ground staff to dry the pitch were _____ fluous.

2 Pick out any spelling errors involving the use of prefixes in the following sentences and correct them.

a The three main points of the presentation were interelated.
b The Prime Minister was reminded of his prelection speech.
c The missunderstandings must be cleared up.
d What a dissappointment the show was!

Further still

Below, there are three examples each of words that use the following five prefixes:

inter-   intro-   pre-   post-   sub-

Explain the effect of the prefix on the stem word and then use each word in a sentence that shows its meaning.

a interjected   intercede   interrelate
b introverted   introductory   introspection
c preordained   preoccupied   preponderance
d postponement   post-natal   post-date
e subcontract   subculture   subdue

Suffixes and their Spellings

A **suffix** is a single letter or a group of letters which, when added to the end of a word, forms another word. For example, *amaze* plus the suffix *-ment* becomes *amazement*; *polite* plus the suffix *-ness* becomes *politeness*.

(See page 40 for more on suffixes and their meanings.)

Suffixes and silent 'e'

Many words in English end with a silent '-e'. This means the 'e' is not pronounced. When you add any suffix to words like this, you need to decide whether to keep the silent 'e' or drop it. What you do depends on whether the suffix itself starts with a consonant or a vowel.

If the suffix begins with a consonant, then the final 'e' is kept:

bereave/bereave*ment*   hope/hope*less*   care/care*ful*

An important exception to this rule is: argue/arg*ument*.

When a suffix beginning with a consonant is added to words ending in '-y', then the 'y' changes to *-i*:

happy/happ*iness*   merry/merr*iness*

But when a suffix begins with a vowel, as in *-ed* or *-ing*, then to avoid two vowels coming together, the final silent 'e' is usually dropped:

come/com*ing*   argue/argu*ing*   rotate/rotat*ed*/rotat*ing*

Note that some monosyllabic words change 'ie' to *-y* before adding *-ing*:

die/d*ying*   lie/l*ying*   tie/t*ying*

(For more on adding *-ed* and *-ing* to verb forms, see page 114.)

Spellings and meanings

1 Adjectives in English often end in *-able* or *-ible* meaning 'able to be'. Here are some of the more common words ending in *-able*:

acceptable   adaptable   adorable   agreeable   forgivable
favourable   unforgettable   honourable   inadvisable

Common words ending in *-ible*:

accessible   legible   illegible   responsible   reversible
feasible   audible   inflexible

2 Some adjectives ending in *-ous* are formed from nouns that end in *-our*, such as *humour*, *glamour*, *vigour*.

But in forming the adjective, the 'u' is dropped and *-ous* added:

humorous   glamorous   vigorous

Other adjectives ending in *-ous* include:

disastrous   jealous   mischievous   enormous   ridiculous

Adjectives that end in *-ious*, *-eous* and *-uous* include:

cautious   anxious   gracious   precious
miscellaneous   advantageous   outrageous   gorgeous
assiduous   deciduous   ambiguous   fatuous

3 Some adjectives ending with -al are:

> political logical postal equal typical numerical
> personal occasional additional critical emotional

4 Some adjectives ending in -ial and -ual are:

> initial essential crucial beneficial jovial ceremonial
> individual annual visual casual continual factual

5 Many nouns describing what someone does for a job end in -er:

> teacher driver joiner lawyer manager hairdresser

Nouns that end in -or are trickier; these include:

> advisor (or adviser) doctor spectator editor governor

Starting point

Add one of the following suffixes to the following words to form another word:

-ment   -ness   -ful   -less

disappoint   grace   lazy   measure   relent   fair
pity   effective   casual   force   loose   fear   arrange
manage   resent   mad   joy

Going further

Read the following article, which contains some spelling errors in the use of suffixes. Rewrite the text correcting the mistakes.

DO YOU TRUST MOST ADVERTISING?

Don't show too much politness when you answer that question. It would be entirely forgiveable if you were distrustfull of most advertisments. We want to see ads that do not go in for lieing, where there's no juggleing with the facts and consumers get real information. Possibley we can bring this about together. It's not a hopeless situation. Of course, not all advertisers can be lumped together. Some ads are created more sincerly than others. Some are even credable. It might be an enormous task, but with your genereous help, it's a crucial job to make advertising dependible and not plain ridiculious.

Further still

Read the following opening to a play. Pick out any spelling errors and then write down the correct version of each word.

Jamal: Let's not be too cautous. We can choose something affordible.
Pippa: Somewhere gorgious. I want this holiday to be unforgettible.
Jamal: I don't want to be responsable for choosing. If it turns out to be disasterous, then you have to take equial blame.
Pippa: I want a luxurous hotel.
Jamal: But not at outragious prices.

Plurals

Creating plural nouns

The most common plural form is created by adding *-s* to the singular noun:

> toy/toys   table/tables   individual/individuals   animal/animals

But there are many exceptions to this. For example, words ending in '-s', '-ss', or '-x' add *-es* to form their plural:

> box/boxes   bus/buses   boss/bosses   loss/losses

Similarly, words ending in '-sh' and '-ch' add *-es* to form their plural:

> match/matches   peach/peaches   wish/wishes   dish/dishes

Nouns ending in '-o'

Nouns ending in '-o' generally form their plural by adding *-es*:

> potato/potatoes   tomato/tomatoes   hero/heroes   echo/echoes

However, this is not always the case:

> piano/pianos   photo/photos   video/videos

Nouns ending in '-y'

If a noun ends with a '-y' with a consonant before it, then the 'y' becomes *-ies* in the plural:

> ally/allies   enemy/enemies   jelly/jellies   lady/ladies
>
> caddy/caddies   melody/melodies   pony/ponies

But nouns ending in '-ey' add only *-s*:

> donkey/donkeys   chimney/chimneys   valley/valleys

Nouns ending in '-fe' and '-f'

Nouns ending in '-fe' and '-f' generally change the 'f' to 'v' and follow this with *-es* in their plural form:

> knife/knives   wife/wives   loaf/loaves   shelf/shelves
>
> leaf/leaves   thief/thieves   scarf/scarves

Notable exceptions to this are:

> roof/roofs   chief/chiefs   grief/griefs

Unusual plurals and compound words

It is as well to be aware of the following unusual plurals that strongly reflect their origins in Latin and Greek:

> crisis/crises   criterion/criteria   stimulus/stimuli

Some words have the same form in the singular and the plural:

> sheep   series   species   mews   innings   means

Compound words, or words with hyphens, usually attach an *-s* to the first word to make their plurals:

> daughter-in-law/daughters-in-law   runner-up/runners-up

Starting point

Form the plural of each of the following words:

building fox pass quantity recess story reach
class army handkerchief beach hoax patio thief
son-in-law

Going further

Some of the plurals used in the following sentences have been wrongly spelt. Rewrite the sentences making the appropriate corrections.

a We took massis of sandwichs, because there was going to be three serieses of games each with two inningses.

b The melodys seemed very familiar with echos from other showes.

c No one could explain the phenomenons of the lights and sounds that many had witnessed in the skys over several Australian beachs.

d The chieves of the peoples met and decided the basies for peace treatys with their enemys.

e Everyone faces several crisises during their lifes.

f The runner-ups received standing ovationes from the crowds.

g Several specieses of animals are under threat.

h The donkies tried to pull the heavy load, but they had to bring in oxes to finish the task.

Further still

Read the following passage in which many plurals are wrongly spelt. Pick these out and correct them.

In most townes and citys there are lots of different types of foods to eat. Sometimes all we want is some baked potatos or sandwichs; at other times we might want to get our tooths into full cooked lunchs. Cookes and chefes have to work long hours and we should see them as heros, keeping us all fed. Parts of their job are less enjoyable – for example, washing dishs, a job that is often given to junior employies. We should celebrate the many varietys of food in our country and all of the opportunitys to eat well.

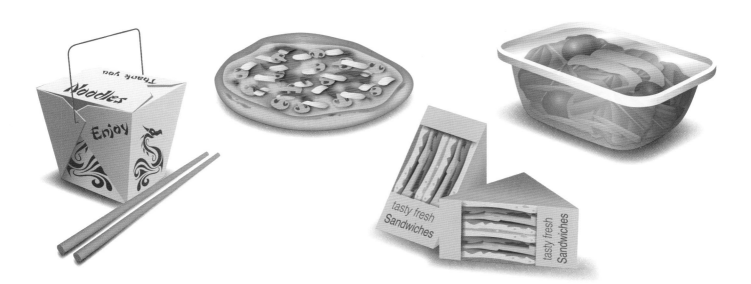

Words that Can Be Confused

Here are 'pairs' of words that are often confused or misspelt. Make sure you know the difference between them and how to spell both.

1	**access**	The slip road meant they had easy *access* to the motel. (verb)
	excess	There was an *excess* in butter production. (noun)
2	**advice**	I gave him good *advice*. (noun)
	advise	He retorted that I had no right to *advise* him. (verb)
3	**affect**	He allowed the tragedy to *affect* him badly. (verb)
	effect	The *effect* of the law was to cut down on crime. (noun)
4	**breath**	They were both very out of *breath* after the race. (noun)
	breathe	It is not easy to *breathe* at high altitude. (verb)
5	**check**	The supervisors had to *check* the quality of the employees' work. (verb)
	cheque	I handed him a *cheque* to pay for it. (noun)
6	**continual**	There was *continual* noise coming from our neighbours. (adjective)
	continuous	The cinema showed *continuous* performances throughout the day. (adjective)
7	**device**	It was a very handy little *device* for hanging pictures. (noun)
	devise	Some designer should *devise* a gadget to do that. (verb)
8	**ensure**	I had to *ensure* that the outcome would be in our favour. (verb)
	insure	On holiday, we had to *insure* ourselves against injury. (verb)
	assure	I do *assure* you there is no truth in that rumour. (verb)
9	**formally**	They were *formally* introduced to the Prime Minister. (adverb)
	formerly	*Formerly*, I worked as a salesperson, but now I am the manager. (adverb)
10	**goal**	My only *goal* is to save enough money to go on holiday. (noun)
	gaol	He was sent to *gaol* for a period of three months. (noun)
11	**licence**	I buy my television *licence* in May every year. (noun)
	license	The council refused to *license* the festival. (verb)
12	**negligent**	The court found that the crew had been *negligent* in their duties. (adjective)
	negligible	The amount of money involved was *negligible*. (adjective)
13	**past**	In the distant *past* there probably was a city called Troy. (noun)
	passed	We *passed* the time by telling tall stories. (verb)
14	**peal**	The *peal* of the bells rang over the city. (noun)
	peel	There is an easy way to *peel* an orange. (verb)

15 **stationary** The vehicle was completely *stationary* when the accident happened. (adjective)

stationery I ordered more *stationery* for use in the office. (noun)

16 **storey** The office was located on the third *storey* of the building. (noun)

story The *story* was fascinating to the listeners. (noun)

Starting point

Identify the words that have been incorrectly used in the following headlines and correct them.

a **The Check that Bounced!**

b **Tell Us Another Storey!**

c **Spurs Breath Easy!**

d **Star Lands in Goal**

e **License Denied to TV Channel!**

f **Explosive Devise Detonated**

Going further

Each one of the following sentences contains at least one example of a word that has been wrongly used because it has been confused with another. Rewrite each sentence using the correct word.

a The newspaper storey affected his personal life greatly.

b If she adviced them to go into the hot desert, she ensured them that this would be negligible of her.

c He made it his gaol to device a plan of action.

d The damage was not negligent, but the drivers excepted responsibility for the accident.

e The woman was not ensured against injury.

f The excess road was totally cut off.

Further still

Read the following opening to a story. Several words have been incorrectly used for their context. Pick out these errors and correct them.

'Our total weight load is in access of what is safe,' the co-pilot said formerly.

'What is your advise then?' asked the captain.

'We must device a plan to off-load so we can be sure of a safe descent. I loathe the idea, but something must be jettisoned.'

'My opinion is that we can land as we are, but I want to assure against any possibility of an accident. What affect will having too much weight on board have?'

'One thing is certain, until the plane is stationery on the runway, we have a problem.'

Tricky Words A–I

Here is a list of words that are tricky to spell. The words on this page run from A–I in the alphabet. Each word is broken down into syllables. Advice on how to remember the correct spelling follows each word.

ab/sence: only *ence* after the *s*
a/ccomm/o/da/tion: double *c* and double *m*
a/cross: one *c* and double *s*
a/ddress: double *d* and double *s*
an/al/y/sis: it's the *y* in the middle and the *-sis* ending
ar/gu/ment: resist the temptation to put an *e* after the *u*
au/tumn: it's the *-mn* at the end

beau/ti/ful: it's *ea* and *ful*
be/ginn/ing: double *n*
be/hav/iour: *iou* at the end
bi/cy/cle: it's *i, c, y* and *c* in that order
busi/ness: the *i* in the middle is scarcely heard

char/act/er: it's the *ch* that gives character to this word
com/par/a/tive/ly: it's *a* before the *tive* syllable
con/science: *science* has *con* before it

def/i/nite: it's definitely *i* in the middle and *-ite* at the end
des/per/ate/ly: three *es* and one *a*
diff/erent: double *f* and one *r*
dis/a/ppoint/ment: one *s* and double *p*
dis/sat/is/fied: double *s* and another one, and *-ied* at the end

eighth: *eight* with *h* added
em/barr/ass: double *r* and double *s* and no embarrassment
en/thus/i/asm: *thus* with *en* before and *-iasm* after
en/viron/ment: it's the *n* before the *m* that is usually left out
ex/agg/er/ate: double *g* followed by an *er*
ex/treme/ly: keep the final *e* of *extreme* and add *-ly*

faith/ful: *-ful* at the end and keep the *faith*
fam/il/iar: add *-iar* to *famil* and this word should look familiar
fav/our/ite: it's *favour* that makes it a favourite
fo/reign: it's like *reign* with *fo* in front
friend: *i* before *e* and you've made friend

govern/ment: it's the *n* before the *m*, as in environment
guar/an/tee: *gu* to begin with then two *as* before the final *-tee*

height: *e* before *i* and then *-ght*

imm/ed/iately: *immediate* plus *-ly*
in/ter/est/ed: *es* all the way
in/terr/upt: double *r* and *upt*
i/sland: that silent *s*

Starting point

Pick out any errors in the following signs.

a Accomodation Available

b Beatiful Flowers For Sale

c Bycicles Repaired

d Protect the Enviroment!

e Goverment in Turmoil

f Buisness For Sale

g Foriegn Currency Exchanged

h Lock your car doors immedately

Going further

Identify the spelling errors in the following sentences and correct them.

a I forgot to tell them my new adress, which was extremly rude of me.

b The buisness at the begining did well, but then suffered from lack of intrest.

c She had a conscence and because of that she was embarased.

d The head was disatisfied with the analisis.

e Comparitively speaking, I am not interrested in the cinema.

f His behaviour was disapointing and only too familar.

Further still

Read the following book report, correcting any spelling errors that you find.

The story is by an extraordinary author, one of my faverites. There can be no arguement about the excitement the story provides or the number of intresting caracters, which manage not to be too familar. An analisis of the plot would take too long, but I garantee you will definately find this a diferent kind of read. The plot is full of beautifull descriptions and there is a complete absense of violence as it reaches a hieght of excitement. I am not exagerating when I say you ought to buy this book imediatly and I am sure you will share my enthuciasm. Take it with you to a desert iland.

Tricky Words J–P

Here is a list of words that are tricky to spell. The words on this page run from J–P in the alphabet. Each word is broken down into syllables. Advice on how to remember the correct spelling follows each word.

jour/ney: *our* not *or*

knife: that silent *k*

lan/guage: it's the *guage* that makes language
length: it's the *-gth* that marks out this word
li/brary: it's *rar* that's the key
lone/ly: add *ly* to *lone*
lone/li/ness: the *-y* beomes *i* and add *-ness*

mag/nif/i/cent: remember two *i*s and a *cent*
marr/iage: double *r* and *-iage* is the key to a good marriage
mar/vell/ous: it's marvellous with a double *l*
misc/ell/an/eous: *s*, *cell* and *-eous*
mys/ter/y: it's a mystery if you use two *y*s

na/ïve: *aï* is the naïve way to do it
nat/ur/all/y: drop the *e* from nature and add *-ally*
nec/ess/ar/y: one *c* and double *s* is absolutely necessary
nec/ess/it/y: one *c*, double *s* and *-ity*
neigh/bours: *e* and *i* are good neighbours
neith/er: *e* before the *i*
nuis/ance: remember *ui* and you'll make a nuisance

o/bed/ient: *obey*, but drop the *-y*, substitute *d* and add *-ient*
o/ccur: double *c* and one *r*
o/ccurr/ed: double the *r* of occur and add *-ed*
of/ten: remember the *t*
o/pin/ion: one *p* and *-ion* and that's an opinion
opp/or/tun/i/ty: double *p*, *ort* and *-unity* gives you an opportunity
or/din/ar/y: *-ary* at the end makes it a very ordinary word
or/i/gin/al: it's the *-al* that makes it original

par/a/llel: three *l*s, with the double after *para*
par/a/ly/sis: drop the *-e* of *paralyse* and add *-is*
parl/ia/ment: remember the *ia* in the middle
part/ic/u/lar: the *-icular* is the *part* to remember
pat/ience: show patience by using the *-ience* ending
pe/cul/iar: it's the *-iar* that makes this slightly peculiar
per/ceive: *e* before *i* after *c* when *ei* sounds like *ee*
per/mis/sion: that *-sion* ending
per/suade: the *ua* in the middle is very persuasive
phys/ic/al: remember that *ph* as *f* sound and it ends in *-al*
pic/ture: picture this word
pop/u/lar: *pop* stars are popular
po/ssess: would you believe it possesses four *s*s?
prej/u/dice: *u* in the middle and *-ice* at the end

prep/ar/a/tion: *prepare* without the *e* and add *-ation*
pres/ence: take a *present*, drop the *t* and add *-ce*
priv/i/lege: *i* in the middle and *-ege* at the end
pro/fess/ion/al: single *f*, double *s*, *ion* and *-al*
psy/chol/o/gy: it's one of the those *-ology* words with *psych-* in front
pur/sue: yes, it is *pur* and it is *-sue*

Starting point

Correct any spelling errors in the following headlines.

a
> # They Were Magnifacent!

b
> # What a Marvelous Surprise!

c
> # Popular Performer Admits Lonliness

d
> # Langage Libary Closed

Going further

Pick out spelling errors in the following sentences and correct them.

a The pupils visted the parlament, which was a rare oportunity.
b The teacher stressed the neccesity to be obedent.
c Every time it ocured, it was a nuisance.
d The neihbours natrally showed patiense about the building work.
e The pictchure is in my opinon orignal.
f I will try to persade her from her pregudice.
g The precense of this pecular pysical being was a mistery.
h It was neccessery to withdraw all priveleges.
i The nife accident thankfully caused no paralisis.

Further still

Correct any spelling errors in the following extract.

Naturlly, the journy was going to be lenthy and lonly. The lonliness was a neccesity because there was no opportunity for more than two people in these particlar circumstances to make the trip. They were not nïave; they knew all sorts of misellaneous difficulties would occurr. They would have to show patence and offen phisical courage.

Their preperashion would have to be meticulous. Niether of them posesed any illusions that it would all be marvelous, but they percieved it as a privelige to go. In the opinons of many experts, they should not have been given permishion. Others had faith in them because of their orginel and professional approach. Success would make them immensely poplar and not at all ordrinary in the future. Such fame might even become a nuisence to them, but they had to see the bigger pichure. They made the paralel with the climbing of Mount Everest for the first time in 1953. They were determined to persue their goal.

Here is a list of words that are tricky to spell. The words on this page run from Q–Z in the alphabet. Each word is broken down into syllables. Advice on how to remember the correct spelling follows each word.

quarr/el: double *r* and single *l*
queue: remember *q- u- e- u- e*

re/al/ize: it's *real* plus *-ize*
re/ceipt: that silent *p* has to be remembered
re/cog/nize: or *recognise* but always with the *recog*
rec/ommend: double *m* is recommended
reg/u/lar/ly: *u* in the middle and *lar* followed by *-ly*
rel/ev/ant: the *ev* and *-ant* are very relevant
re/sem/blance: it's *resemble* without the final *e* and with *-ance*
re/spons/i/bil/it/y: think *ability*, drop the *a*, add *i* and *respons* at the front
rest/aur/ant: it's the *aur* that makes it a good restaurant
rhyme: it's the *rhy* that makes it rhyme
rhy/thm: take *rhy* and *-thm* and you've got rhythm
rid/ic/u/lous: *u* and the *-lous* makes it ridiculous

sci/ence: *sci* plus *-ence*
sec/ret/ar/y: it's *secret* plus *-ary*
sep/ar/ate: yes, *ar* in the middle and *-ate* at the end
ser/ies: *-ies* makes it a series
sim/il/ar/ly: it's *similar* but with *-ly* added
sin/cere/ly: it's *sincere* plus *-ly*
skil/ful: one *l* in the middle and at the end makes you skilful
straight: *-aight* takes you straight to the mark
strength: *-gth* gives you strength
sub/tle: the silent *b* is very subtle
suc/ceed: double *c* and double *e* and you succeed
suc/cess/ful: double *c* and double *s* and you're successful
sur/prise: it's the first *r* that's the surprise

taught: teach yourself the *-aught*
tech/nique: to have technique, you add *-nique* to *tech*
tem/per/a/ture: you take *temper* and you add *-ature*
tem/por/ar/y: *por* and *-ary* makes it temporary
thea/tre: *ea* and *-tre* makes a show of it
thor/ough: *or* and *-ough* makes it thorough
to/morr/ow: double *r* and *ow* and tomorrow comes
twel/fth: the funny *-fth* sound

un/nec/ess/ar/y: double *n*, single *c*, double *s* and *-ary*
us/u/al/ly: *ual* not just usually but always

val/u/able: the *ua* in the middle
var/i/ous: *-ious* word

weigh: remember *ei* makes weigh
wel/come: one *l* plus *come*
writt/en: it needs a double *t*

Starting point

Pick out any spelling errors in the following and correct them.

a
Restarant
Closed
on Saturdays

b
Secretery
Needed
Apply Within

c
Ridiculos Safty
Standards Adopted

d
New Radio
Sereis Starts on
twelth of June

e
High Tempratures
For Tuesday

f
Scienece
For A Sucessful
Tomorow

Going further

Identify the spelling errors in the following sentences and correct them.

a I relized it was only skilfull propaganda and not at all relavant.
b The thetre play was ritten a long time ago.
c The poem had rythm and ryme, and was in seperate verses.
d I recommend you speak sincerly and strait at the audience.
e The resemblence is suttle but welcom.
f Usally, it is unecesary to book for this thetre.
g I would recomend varous and thorugh technicks.
h My timetable included going to an after-scool gym club.
i The restarant divided customers into separate quues.
j I relaised I had not had a receit for last Wednesday.

Further still

Read the following article, picking out the many spelling errors it contains and correcting them.

Psychology Online

Psychology is a modern sience, which people pursue because of its valable insights. Its strenth is that it helps people relise truths about themselves and, therefore, to face up to responsiblties. However, some people claim it is not relevent and does not add to the overall welfare of individuals. Yet, in many scools nowadays, psychology is taugt sucesfully. Simlarly, in universities, it suceeds in attracting a suprising number of students. They reconise the suttle tecnics that this science teaches.

Sample Test 1

You have 50 minutes to write your answers. You are advised to spend approximately:

- 10 minutes on Section A (Spelling)
- 10 minutes on Section B (Punctuation)
- 10 minutes on Section C (Grammar)
- 10 minutes on Section D (Grammar and Punctuation).

Check through your work carefully in the final 5–10 minutes.

Section A: Spelling

The text below is about science-fiction films. There are some spelling errors in the text. They are printed in **bold**. Write down the correct spelling for each of these words.

The (1) **amasing** (2) **sucess** of science-fiction films continues to grow and grow. Most of these movies have American directors and (3) **there** latest offering is now breaking box-office records in twenty (4) **countrys**.

Naturally, the launch of these films and the rewards (5) **reeped** by the film industry are not (6) **accidentle**. Film (7) **exctives** have been (8) **planing** this (9) **stratigy** and it has (10) **certanaly** paid off in terms of mass (11) **poplarity**.

But these films, and the way they have been marketed, have come in for more than their fair share of (12) **critisisim**. (13) **unfortunatley**, many of these comments have come from within the industry itself.

(13 marks)

Section B: Punctuation

The article below is about cinema-going. The article has some punctuation marks in place. However, others are missing and this makes the meaning hard to understand in places.

Read the article through carefully. Then rewrite it, inserting the missing punctuation marks where you think they should go to make the meaning clear. You should include:

- capital letters
- full stops
- question marks
- commas
- apostrophes
- inverted commas (speech marks).

The first paragraph has been done for you.

Going to the Cinema

Going to the cinema is more than just about seeing a film. Don't you get more from the experience of cinema-going than just seeing a movie?

What more is involved Well it is an experience you share with the other people in the audience. it is quite a different experience from watching films in your own home. there is something about an audience that is really enjoying a movie that heightens your own enjoyment.

Films are meant to be seen on the big screen. A film such as *avatar* can only really be appreciated when it is shown on a giant screen. steven spielberg the famous hollywood director has been quoted as saying im in the business of creating fantasy.

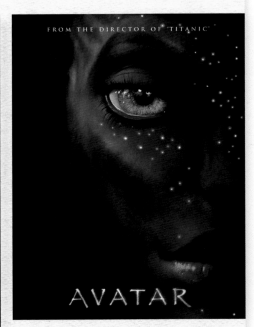

The locations the special effects the camerawork the costumes and the stars themselves all gain from being projected onto a larger-than-life screen and create this fantasy world. Its a magical world, isnt it

(12 marks)

Section C: Grammar

Read this letter written to a newspaper and then answer the questions that follow it.

Less Violence on Our Screens!

Dear Sir,

1   There has been a notable increase in the level of violence in films over the last ten years. In the past, during what some people refer to as the 'golden age of the cinema', films were made that only suggested violence, but they did not openly show it in the same way that contemporary films do. Films were more heavily censored then, of course, and film-makers were obliged to meet tighter standards. It could be argued that the increase in violent films is dictated by the changing tastes of film audiences. But what comes first – the chicken or the egg? Is it audience taste or film-makers' own wishes to make violent films?

10 I feel strongly that films that contain explicit violence can be harmful. I would argue they might even lead to 'copycat' acts of violence. I know that not everybody would agree with me on this and I am certainly not arguing for wholesale censorship of films. Unfortunately, there is violence in real life and films must reflect that to a certain extent. But in my opinion it is a matter of degree and things have now gone far too far. What then can we cinema-goers do about it? Although we should stop paying our money to see films that exploit violent scenes, we need to let our voices be heard by expressing our opinions in public, by writing to important people and by influencing our friends. Let's see some less

20 violent films!

---

1   The writer has not used paragraphs in the above letter.

   a Decide where you would start *one* new paragraph by writing the first few words of the sentence that would begin this new paragraph.

   b Explain why a new paragraph should start at this point, using the letter to support what you say. You could start your answer with these words:

     I started a new paragraph at this point because…   *(2 marks)*

2   The letter uses passive verb forms at the beginning and active verb forms in the second half. For example:

Passive	**Active**
films were made (line 3)	I would argue (line 11)
film-makers were obliged (line 6)	they might even lead (line 11)

How does the change from the passive to the active form contribute to the development of the arguments put forward in the letter?   *(2 marks)*

3 The writer uses *I* and *we* (first person singular and plural) in the second half of the letter, whereas in the first half these personal pronouns are not used. Why do you think the writer makes this change?   *(2 marks)*

4 In this letter the writer often combines several ideas into one sentence. For example, here are some notes for the first draft:

- Films were different in the golden age of the cinema.
- Violence was only suggested.
- It was rarely openly shown.
- Contemporary films show more violence.

In the final draft these have been joined into a single sentence:

> In the past, during what some people refer to as the 'golden age of the cinema', films were made that only suggested violence, but they did not openly show it in the same way that contemporary films do.

Below are some sentences which the writer did not include in the final draft of the letter. Join the ideas into *one* sentence. Use connectives (linking words and phrases) and correct punctuation. You can, of course, change the order of the ideas if you wish:

- Many people argue a different point of view.
- There is more violence nowadays.
- Films only reflect that trend.
- This is inevitable.   *(2 marks)*

5 This sentence comes near the end of the letter on lines 16–19. Read it again:

> Although we should stop paying our money to see films that exploit violent scenes, we need to let our voices be heard by expressing our opinions in public, by writing to important people and by influencing our friends.

The sentence has a main clause, two subordinate clauses and three phrases.

a Write down the main clause of the sentence.   *(1 mark)*
b How does the way that the three phrases are written emphasize the main idea of the sentence?   *(2 marks)*

6 The long sentence studied in question 5 is followed by the last sentence in the article. This is very short and has no subordinate clauses. How does the structure of each of the last two sentences contribute to the writer's arguments?   *(2 marks)*

(Total: 13 marks)

135

Section D: Grammar and Punctuation

The following notes describe the history of the cinema. Read the notes carefully.

The History of the Cinema

Paragraph 1 {

- 1895: the Lumière brothers' first showing of films in a public cinema in Paris

- Early cinemas called 'nickelodeons'; by 1907, over 3000 nickelodeons across America

- In the 1920s, major film studios are well-established in Hollywood

- Film-makers in the rest of the world compete for audiences with the Americans

- Favourite film stars attract millions of fans to the cinema

- 1927: the end of silent films with the coming of sound; *The Jazz Singer* the first sound film

- Studios all round the world; production of sound films only

- 1930s and 1940s: the continuing growth of the film business with Hollywood films the most popular round the world

- 1950s: the coming of television and the decline in attendances at cinemas

- Hollywood: epic films projected onto wide screens to meet challenge of television

- Mostly young people under 25 who go to the cinema regularly

- The arrival and spread of multi-screen cinemas

- The next competition for cinema: films on DVD and illegal downloads via the Internet; people watch new films at home

- New challenges to cinema owners to attract audiences to their cinemas

Paragraph 5

- The future of cinema: new technology, e.g. 3D, Pixar animation; multi-screens with additional attractions, e.g. armchairs, bar service; 'home' cinema, films on a 'pay-as-you-view' basis

Using the notes on page 136, write the rest of this account of how the cinema developed, showing how the different stages of its history are connected. Paragraphs 1 and 5 have been done for you. Write paragraphs 2, 3 and 4, based closely on the notes and using the following as a guide.

In your writing remember to:

- write sentences with more than one idea and use connectives (linking words or phrases)
- group the notes into an order which helps you avoid repetition
- use accurate grammar and punctuation.

Paragraph 1

In 1895, the Lumière brothers were responsible for the first public showing of films in a cinema. This took place in Paris, but soon the early form of cinemas, the 'nickelodeons', grew in number; by 1907, there were 3000 nickelodeons across America alone.

Paragraph 5

What, then, will the future of the cinema be? We have already seen technological developments, such as Pixar animation and 3D, and new technology will certainly continue to dazzle audiences. Cinema owners will provide additional attractions, such as armchairs and a drinks service. At the same time, 'home' cinema will continue to spread, with people watching films on a 'pay-as-you-view' basis.

(12 marks)

Sample Test 2

Section A: Spelling

The text below is about animals in captivity. There are some spelling errors in the text. They are printed in **bold**. Write down the correct spelling for each of these words.

There are (1) **maney** differing (2) **opinons** about animals kept in captivity. Millions of people see nothing (3) **rong** in zoos, safari parks and (4) **numerus** other attractions where animals are confined.

However, animals need only to be seen in their natural (5) **enviroment** for people to (6) **relaize** how (7) **artifical** and constricting these places are for wild animals. In the wild, animals can (8) **rome** as they wish and they are not (9) **dependant** on human beings to feed and care for them.

It is true that in captivity wild animals are safe from danger from other (10) **speces**, but there is something rather sad about an (11) **elefant**, for example, in a confined space in a zoo. Even in a safari park, where there is (12) **generaly** more room for the animals to roam; lions and tigers (13) **frequentley** look bored.

(13 marks)

Section B: Punctuation

The article below is about animal rights. The article has some punctuation marks in place. However, others are missing and this makes the meaning hard to understand in places.

Read the article through carefully. Then rewrite it, putting the punctuation marks where you think they should go to make the meaning clear. You should include:

- capital letters
- full stops
- question marks
- commas
- apostrophes
- inverted commas (speech marks).

The first paragraph has been done for you.

Animal Rights

INFO **CONTACT**

We hear much about animal rights these days. Indeed, groups of very committed people make sure that the issue of animal rights is never far from the headlines.

Why, then should we think that animal rights are so important human beings are surely more important and many human rights have still to be fought for. however, its not a matter of choosing between the two. Both humans and animals have rights.

A spokesperson for an animal rights group, Margaret jones who, incidentally, does not believe in violent action, has stated: i believe that animals have just as much right to be treated well here on this earth as human beings. we simply do not have the right to exploit them. Yet why is it we mistreat them so often she added.

nevertheless there are opponents arguments that have to be put experiments on animals have probably saved the lives of millions of people. can such experiments ever be justified The idea that animals should suffer for our sakes is abhorrent to many people as it is to the rspca the organization that protects animals it is a complicated question and one that will not be solved overnight.

(12 marks)

Section C: Grammar

Read this letter written to a local newspaper and then answer the questions that follow it.

Save The Mirimar Pop Festival!

Dear Editor,

1 It has been proposed that the local council refuse a licence to the organizers of the pop music festival that has taken place in Mirimar Park for the last three years in July. The Mirimar Festival was developed by local enthusiasts, who were encouraged by the response of local young people to the first event, to expand its scope with the result that well-known groups have since been invited and have been enjoyed by large audiences. Its reputation as a first-rate music festival has been established. However, now the renewal of its licence has been opposed by local residents and the council has been pressured to give in. I am

10 appalled by this decision. I do not understand what the local residents have to complain about. The music finishes at nine in the evening and the main site is at some distance from any houses. Of course, there will be a certain amount of noise that will be heard by local residents, but would they be complaining, say, if the music was a classical concert? Those of us who have enjoyed all three festivals must protest at this move to kill off this event, which has proved so popular with many local young people. We must make our views heard and we must write to our local councillors. We should be organizing a petition for the public to sign, which I think many people of different ages would do, as it is

20 generally agreed that crowds at the festival have been well-behaved and the site itself has been cleared up adequately. Let's save our pop festival!

---

1 The writer has not used paragraphs in the above letter.
  a Decide where you think *one* new paragraph should begin by writing down the first few words of the sentence that would begin this new paragraph.
  b Explain why a new paragraph should start at this point, using the letter to support what you say. You could start your answer with these words:

  I started a new paragraph at this point because…   *(2 marks)*

2 The letter uses passive verb forms at the beginning and active verb forms in the second half. For example:

Passive	Active
It has been proposed (line 1)	I do not understand (line 10)
The Mirimar Festival was developed (line 3)	Those of us who have enjoyed (line 15)

How does the change from the passive to the active form contribute to the development of the arguments in the letter?   *(2 marks)*

3 The writer uses *I* (first person singular) for some of the letter. The end of the letter, from line 15, is written using mainly *we* and *us* (first person plural). Why do you think the writer makes this change? *(2 marks)*

4 In this letter the writer often combines several ideas in one sentence. For example, here are some notes for the first draft of the letter:

- Mirimar Festival developed by local enthusiasts.
- Encouraged by response of young people to first festival.
- Expanded the scope of the event.
- Since invited popular well-known bands.

In the final draft, these have been joined into a single sentence:

> The Mirimar Festival was developed by local enthusiasts, who were encouraged by the response of local young people to the first event, to expand its scope with the result that well-known groups have since been invited and have been enjoyed by large audiences.

Below are some sentences which the writer did not include in the final draft of the letter. Join the ideas into *one* sentence. Use connectives (linking words and phrases) and correct punctuation. You can, of course, change the order of the ideas if you wish:

- There is a lack of pop concerts in this area.
- Mirimar Park is an excellent site for such an event.
- It is large and reasonably far from local housing estates.
- The event would attract young people and business to the area.

(2 marks)

5 Read this sentence again which comes from lines 15–17:

> Those of us who have enjoyed all three festivals must protest at this move to kill off this event, which has proved so popular with many local young people.

This sentence has a main clause and two subordinate clauses.

a Write down the main clause in the sentence. *(1 mark)*
b Write down both the subordinate clauses. *(2 marks)*

6 The penultimate sentence of the letter consists of a main clause and four subordinate clauses. The last sentence is, by contrast, very short and has no subordinate clauses. How does the structure of each of the last two sentences contribute to the writer's arguments? *(2 marks)*

(Total: 13 marks)

Section D: Grammar and Punctuation   The following notes describe the rise in popularity of rock and pop music. Read the notes carefully.

The Rise of Rock and Pop

Paragraph 1

- Pop music really started in the mid-1950s with rock and roll
- Rock and roll groups such as Bill Haley and the Comets: huge record hits
- Elvis Presley major rock star: concerts and records
- Rock and roll seen as 'dangerous' to begin with by many older people
- The audience for rock and roll grew incredibly; took over the pop music scene
- Soul music and rhythm and blues music part of rock
- 1960s: famous groups such as The Beatles and the Rolling Stones
- Individual singers such as Marvin Gaye and Tina Turner highly successful
- Several strands to rock music including more commercial music as well as more serious experimental rock
- Huge rock concerts usual in the 1960s
- Individual performers and pop groups enormously famous and rich
- A reaction against 'distant' rock stars; 'punk rock' born
- Punk rock: a challenge to the 'glamour' and 'phoniness' of some of the rock music industry
- Some of these punk rock stars: huge rock stars themselves

Paragraph 5

- Since 1980, rock music has continued to flourish
- Sales of CDs made record companies prosperous but more difficult now that music easy to download from the Internet
- Rock concerts still popular; also music festivals held all over UK and Europe which attract huge crowds
- Rock music here to stay but bound to change

Using the notes on page 142, write the rest of this account of the development of rock and pop music. Paragraphs 1 and 5 have been done for you. Write paragraphs 2, 3 and 4, based closely on the notes and using the following as a guide.

In your writing remember to:

- write sentences with more than one idea and use connectives (linking words or phrases)
- group the notes into an order which helps you avoid repetition
- use accurate grammar and punctuation.

Paragraph 1

Pop music really started in the mid-1950s, when rock and roll groups, such as Bill Haley and the Comets, had huge record hits and Elvis Presley became a major star through records and concerts. However, rock and roll was seen as 'dangerous' to begin with by many older people.

Paragraph 5

Nevertheless, since 1980, rock music has continued to flourish, because the sale of CDs made record companies prosperous. Things, however, are constantly changing. Although rock concerts are still popular and music festivals attract huge crowds, it is easy now to download music from the Internet and share it with friends. Rock music is here to stay but will have to change.

(12 marks)

Sample Test 3

Section A: Spelling

The text below is about sport. There are some spelling errors in the text. They are printed in **bold**. Write down the correct spelling for each of these words.

It has (1) **offen** been said that we have become a nation of (2) **spectaters** as far as sport is concerned. Professional sport has become such big (3) **buisness** and is watched by so many millions of people, especially on (4) **telvision**, that perhaps we are in danger of being armchair sportsmen and (5) **wimmen**.

Surely there has to be a balance between taking part in sport and watching other people, who are (6) **usally** being paid, perform for us. There is nothing wrong with being a fan of a particular sport and following your (7) **favrite** team, but can being a member of a crowd ever take the place of actually taking part in a sport?

This is an important question at a time when so much lottery money is being given to sport. It is (8) **necesary** to (9) **encorage** individuals to (10) **particepate** in sport as well as giving grants to official bodies. It is (11) **particlarly** important that young people take part: sport is a (12) **helthy** (13) **passtime**.

(13 marks)

Section B: Punctuation

The article below is about sports facilities for young people and the disabled. The article has some punctuation marks. However, others are missing and this makes the meaning hard to understand at times.

Read the article through. Then rewrite it, putting in the missing punctuation marks where you think they should go to make the meaning clear. You should include:

- capital letters
- full stops
- question marks
- commas
- apostrophes
- inverted commas (speech marks).

The first paragraph has been done for you.

Time for Change in Sports Provision

A special case must be made for the provision of sports facilities for young people and the disabled. Too often both categories have lost out when it comes to the allocation of cash from the government and other organizations.

its simply a matter of fairness,' claims norman Jones secretary of one of the leading sports bodies because too much has been given in the past to adult sport many other people voice the same opinions as Jones.

How can fairness in the giving of grants be ensured certainly those who give out grants must be aware of the needs of both groups. The national lottery has immense power in this area and those who decide where lottery money goes have to think about special facilities specialist coaching access location and many other factors.

Fortunately there is a lot of cash available for sport at present, television revenues have been a boon to many sports. Jackie brown, who works for an important pressure group for sport states, 'i am very hopeful. This is a good time for sport all round, including for the young and the disabled.

(12 marks)

Section C: Grammar Read this letter written to a newspaper and then answer the questions that follow it.

The Joys of Being a Fan!

Dear Editor,

1 Fans are often portrayed as being slightly odd people. Fans of all types, of sport, music, films, theatre and all sorts of other entertainments, are frequently described as being even slightly crazy. Why have fans been landed with this reputation? Surely there is nothing wrong with being an enthusiastic follower of something or someone that really interests you? Of course, there are fans who take things to extremes by devoting all their time to fan worship, by spending all their money on their particular fanaticism and by neglecting important things in their life. Perhaps this minority of fans lack something in their lives, a gap which they are trying

10 to fill through their enthusiasm for this one pursuit, whether it be football, pop music or whatever, which they hope will give their life extra meaning. But most fans do not fit into this category of fanatic and manage to keep their enthusiasm within some kind of bounds. I and most of my friends are keen followers of our local football team. We see all their home matches, of course, and occasionally we manage to travel to see away matches as well. We all admit that how our team fares each week affects how we feel till the next match. In addition, most of us would say that sometimes it matters too much by depressing us when the results are bad, by letting this affect our relationships and by devoting too much

20 time to supporting the team. Still, here's to being a fan!

1 The writer has not used paragraphs in the above letter.
   a Show where *one* new paragraph should begin by writing down the first few words of the sentence that would begin this new paragraph.
   b Explain why a new paragraph should start at this point, using the letter to support what you say. You could start your answer with these words:

   I started a new paragraph at this point because...   *(2 marks)*

2 The letter contains passive verb forms at the beginning and active verb forms in the second half. For example:

Passive	**Active**
Fans are often portrayed (line 1)	We see all their home matches (line 14)
Why have fans been landed (line 3)	We all admit (line 16)

How does the change from the passive to the active form contribute to the development of the writer's arguments?   *(2 marks)*

3 The writer uses *I* and *we* (first person singular and plural) in the second part of the letter, but not in the first part. Why do you think the writer makes this change? *(2 marks)*

4 In this letter the writer often combines several ideas into one sentence. For example, here are some notes for the first draft:

- Minority of fans perhaps lack something in their lives.
- They try to fill the gap with their particular enthusiasm.
- It does not matter what that enthusiasm is.
- They hope it will give their lives extra meaning.

In the final draft these have been joined into a single sentence:

Perhaps this minority of fans lack something in their lives, a gap which they are trying to fill through their enthusiasm for this one pursuit, whether it be football, pop music or whatever, which they hope will give their life extra meaning.

Below are some sentences which the writer did not include in the final draft of the letter. Join the ideas into *one* sentence. Use connectives (linking words and phrases) and correct punctuation. You can, of course, change the order of the ideas if you wish:

- Fan worship can easily be made fun of.
- Not everybody understands the reasons.
- People not involved can be resentful.
- Fans can put their interest before everything and everyone.

(2 marks)

5 This sentence comes in lines 6–8 of the letter. Read it again:

Of course, there are fans who take things to extremes by devoting all their time to fan worship, by spending all their money on their particular fanaticism and by neglecting important things in their life.

This sentence has a main clause, a subordinate clause and three phrases.

  a Write down the main clause in the sentence.   *(1 mark)*
  b How does the way that the three phrases are written emphasize the main idea of fans taking things to extremes?   *(2 marks)*

6 The long sentence which is the second last sentence of the letter is followed by a very short last sentence. How does the structure of each of these sentences contribute to their effect?   *(2 marks)*

(Total: 13 marks)

Section D: Grammar and Punctuation

The following notes describe the growth of professional sport. Read the notes carefully.

Professional Sport Old and New

Paragraph 1

- Professional sport a comparatively recent development

- In the nineteenth century, emergence of professionals in football, boxing, cricket and other sports

- Some sports stars household names

- Financial rewards relatively small by present-day standards

- Link between the growth of mass communications and growth of professional sport

- Newspapers: pages of sports reports

- Increase in number of mass spectator sports: a world-wide phenomenon

- Events such as the Olympic Games and World Cup football

- The televising of sport and huge increase in public interest

- Satellite broadcasts: sport from around the world on offer

- Professional sport now very big business

- One result: huge financial rewards for superstars of sport

- Ending of amateur-professional divide in other sports, such as rugby and athletics

Paragraph 4

- Some people against wholesale commercialization of sport

- Money more important than taking part

- Winning at all cost; so much at stake

- With the growth and vast interest in professional sport come problems

Using the notes on page 148, write the rest of this account of the growth of professional sport. Paragraphs 1 and 4 have been done for you. Write paragraphs 2 and 3, based closely on the notes and using the following as a guide.

In your writing remember to:

- write sentences with more than one idea and use connectives (linking words or phrases)
- group the notes into an order which helps you avoid repetition
- use accurate grammar and punctuation.

Paragraph 1

Professional sport has been a comparatively recent development. However, in the nineteenth century, there did emerge many professionals in sports such as football, boxing, cricket and other sports. Some of these professional sports stars became household names even then, but the financial rewards for these individuals were relatively small by present-day standards.

Paragraph 4

Some people deplore this wholesale commercialization of sport because they believe it has led to money being more important than taking part. It has also encouraged an attitude of winning at all cost, because so much is now at stake. There is no doubt that with the growth and vast interest in professional sport come attendant problems.

(12 marks)

Sample Test 4

You have 50 minutes to write your answers. You are advised to spend approximately:

- 10 minutes on Section A (Spelling)
- 10 minutes on Section B (Punctuation)
- 10 minutes on Section C (Grammar)
- 10 minutes on Section D (Grammar and Punctuation).

Check through your work carefully in the final 5–10 minutes.

Section A: Spelling

The text below is about making collections. There are some spelling errors in the text. They are highlighted in **bold**. Write down the correct spelling for each of these words.

Many adults and young people are collectors of all kinds of things: stamps, toys, dolls, comics, (1) **magasines** and many other categories. With some people, old and young alike, it can become an (2) **obsesion**.

Why do people want to make a collection of something they are (3) **interrested** in? Firstly, it is the fact that they enjoy a particular (4) **hobbey**. From this interest comes the desire to (5) **aquire** other things associated with it.

There is nothing (6) **harmfull** in this, of course, unless collectors start to spend all their money on their collection. Collectors find their thrills in the (7) **suden** (8) **discoverys** of (9) **tresures** that only they seem to know the value of and which leave the rest of us puzzled.

From dinky toys to CDs, the range of such collections is vast. Each collector protects his or her own (10) **seperate** collection, (11) **weather** it be stamps or old comics. Some become very keen to 'complete' their collection and will not rest until they have (12) **acheived** that. However, once the collection is completed, what do they do then? Perhaps start a (13) **diffrent** type of collection altogether!

(13 marks)

Section B: Punctuation

The article below is about comics. The article has some punctuation marks in place. However, others are missing and this makes the meaning hard to understand in places.

Read the article through. Then rewrite it, putting in the missing punctuation marks where you think they should go to make the meaning clear. You should include:

- capital letters
- full stops
- question marks
- commas
- apostrophes
- inverted commas (speech marks).

The first paragraph has been done for you.

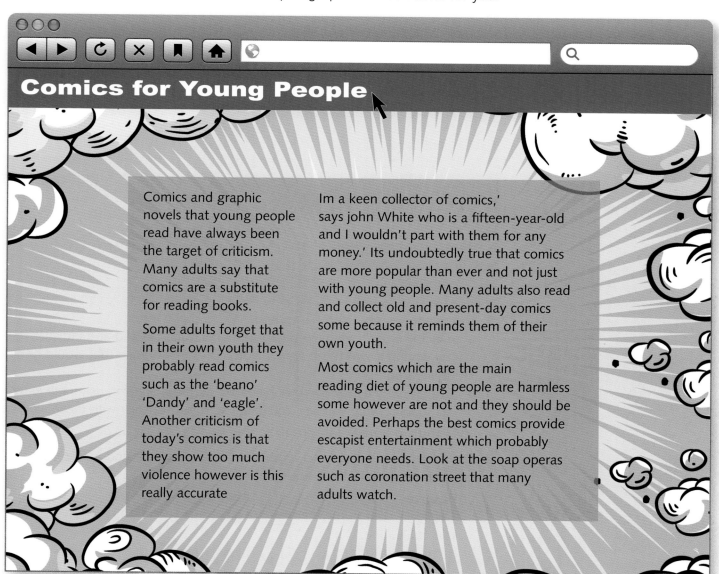

Comics for Young People

Comics and graphic novels that young people read have always been the target of criticism. Many adults say that comics are a substitute for reading books.

Some adults forget that in their own youth they probably read comics such as the 'beano' 'Dandy' and 'eagle'. Another criticism of today's comics is that they show too much violence however is this really accurate

Im a keen collector of comics,' says john White who is a fifteen-year-old and I wouldn't part with them for any money.' Its undoubtedly true that comics are more popular than ever and not just with young people. Many adults also read and collect old and present-day comics some because it reminds them of their own youth.

Most comics which are the main reading diet of young people are harmless some however are not and they should be avoided. Perhaps the best comics provide escapist entertainment which probably everyone needs. Look at the soap operas such as coronation street that many adults watch.

(12 marks)

Section C: Grammar   Read this letter written to a local newspaper and then answer the questions that follow.

Save Our Community Centre!

Dear Editor

1   The local community centre was built over twenty years ago. It has been funded ever since by our local council and its facilities have been enjoyed by both young and old for all that time. It has been firmly established as a focal point for our community. There has been a recent proposal that the centre should no longer be funded by the council. It has been stated that cuts have to be made in the local budget and that the closing down of the centre would be advantageous. No consultation has been undertaken by the council, which many local residents are angered by, because this council has always boasted that it always consults people, a

10 fact which clearly is not true in this case. I and many other young people are amazed at the move to close the centre. I have used its sports and leisure facilities many times and I had been looking forward to doing so for many years to come. The centre is very special for me, because I spent a good deal of my younger years there, enjoying myself with my friends or my parents. Many of us are of the opinion that we must do something to stop this closure. After all, the council is supposed to listen to what we want, which is very definitely to ensure that this valuable community asset remains open. What, then, can we do? We can write to our MP, who is sympathetic to our cause, and we can raise public

20 awareness by airing the issue whenever possible, by writing again to the local newspaper and by asking people to sign a petition. We need to make our voices heard!

1 The writer has not used paragraphs in the above letter.
   a Decide where *one* new paragraph should be started and indicate this by writing down the first few words of the sentence that would begin this paragraph.
   b Explain why a new paragraph should start at this point, using the letter to support what you say. You could start your answer with these words:

   I started a new paragraph at this point because…   *(2 marks)*

2 The letter contains passive verb forms in the first half and active verb forms in second half. For example:

Passive	**Active**
The local community centre was built (line 1)	I have used (line 11)
It has been funded (line 1)	I spent a good deal of… (line 14)

How does the change from the passive to the active form contribute to the development of the letter overall?   *(2 marks)*

3 The writer uses *I* and *we* (first person singular and plural) in the second part of this letter. Why do you think the writer starts to use the first person in this way? *(2 marks)*

4 In this letter, the writer often combines several ideas into one sentence. For example, here are some notes for the first draft:

- No consultation by council
- Local residents angry
- Council's boast it always consults
- Not in this case

In the final letter, these have been combined into one sentence:

No consultation has been undertaken by the council, which many local residents are angered by, because this council has always boasted that it always consults people, a fact which is clearly not true in this case.

Below are some sentences which the writer did not include in the final version of the letter. Join the ideas into *one* sentence. Use connectives (linking words and phrases) and correct punctuation. You can, of course, change the order of the ideas if you wish:

- Before the centre was opened, there were no leisure facilities.
- A campaign by local people highlighted this problem.
- The campaign was supported by the council.
- The council wished to provide leisure facilities for the young.

(2 marks)

5 The sentence below comes near the end of the letter on lines 18–21.

We can write to our MP, who is sympathetic to our cause, and we can raise public awareness by airing the issue whenever possible, by writing again to the local newspaper and by asking people to sign a petition.

This sentence has two main clauses, two subordinate clauses, and three phrases.
a Write down *one* of the main clauses. *(1 mark)*
b Write down *one* of the subordinate clauses. *(1 mark)*
c How does the way that the three phrases are written emphasize the point about raising public awareness? *(1 mark)*

6 The long sentence studied in question 5 is followed by the last sentence of the letter. This is very short. How does the structure of each of the last two sentences contribute to the writer's arguments? *(2 marks)*

(Total: 13 marks)

Sample Test 4 Continued

Section D: Grammar and Punctuation

The following notes describe how field and ice hockey grew in popularity from their beginnings as sports. Read the notes below carefully.

The History of Hockey

Paragraph 1

- Hockey: a game played on a field or on ice
- Field hockey: eleven-a-side game
- Played with a ball and sticks
- All sorts of rules about hitting the ball
- Field hockey first developed in England
- Became popular in the 1870s
- Became an Olympic event in 1908
- Played all over the world by both men and women
- Mainly amateur sport but with some professionals
- Ice hockey: six-a-side game played with a rubber puck and sticks
- Developed in Canada in the 1870s
- Particularly popular in 'cold' countries
- Very fast sport: tough and dangerous
- Professional teams in America and Canada compete in leagues
- Professional ice hockey has developed quickly in Britain in last twenty years
- A fiercely-contested Olympic event
- Field hockey and ice hockey: different skills
- Ice hockey: skill at ice skating paramount
- Danger of serious injury: players heavily protected

Paragraph 4

- Field hockey slower but very skilful game
- The men's and women's game receive good coverage
- Men's and women's hockey games frequently televised

Using the notes on page 154, write the rest of this account of the history of hockey. Paragraphs 1 and 4 have been done for you. Write paragraphs 2 and 3, based closely on the notes and using the following as a guide.

In your writing remember to:

- write sentences with more than one idea and use connectives (linking words or phrases)
- group the notes into an order which helps you avoid repetition
- use accurate grammar and punctuation.

Paragraph 1

Hockey is a game that is played either on a field or on ice. Field hockey is an eleven-a-side game, in which the players use a ball and sticks. In addition, there are all sorts of rules connected with hitting the ball.

Paragraph 4

Field and ice hockey require different skills. Whereas in ice hockey, there is the danger of serious injury and players are heavily protected, skill at ice-skating is paramount; field hockey is a slower but equally skilful game. Men's hockey and women's hockey, which are frequently televised, receive good coverage.

(12 marks)

Index